UNIVERSAL ACCLAIM FOR

HOW TO SELL
Clear and Simple

"Many people have bought into the idea that good salespeople are born and cannot be trained. This book definitely reverses that concept."

Jean Gonsalves, Executive Director, Actionwise, South Africa

• • •

"An excellent overall book that covers all the basics of selling in an easy to follow and understand manner."

Larry Silver, President and Owner, Hollander Consultants

• • •

"I enjoyed this book tremendously. It takes the sales process and makes it simple. Read this book and find out just how easy and fun sales can be—when done in this friendly, win-win way."

Shaun Kirk, Physical Therapist and President, Measurable Solutions

• • •

"The tools of selling – basic, vital, complete. Easily understood for application."

Jerry Langenfeld, Senior Vice President, Sterling Management Systems

Continued. . .

"Examples for each principle and procedure, many laced with humor, lend a light and refreshing aspect to this very practical book."

Mike Campbell, National Sales Manager, Cost Redux

• • •

"*HOW TO SELL* is ready to use. It is easy to read and will be put to immediate use in our company. It is an important addition to any sales library, and very useful in training and advanced training sessions."

Jim Mathers, President and National Sales Manager,
Consumer Energy Solutions, Inc.

• • •

"If you want successful sales and happy customers, read and use this book. It is easy to understand and gives the reader the simple yet powerful tools of sales. It is not filled with gimmicks or tricks to get someone to buy. It explains how to use real tools based on communication and understanding to help prospects overcome their barriers when making a purchase."

Lyle Cunningham, Senior Vice President of Sales,
David Singer Enterprises

• • •

"This book opened my eyes to what has been working, and what I *should* have been applying, over my last ten years in sales. It can help anyone, from the new salesman to the experienced pro. I suggest you read and use it."

Istvan Holbok, Sales Consultant and Lecturer, COMLINE Budapest

• • •

HOW TO SELL

Clear and Simple

by
Harry Frisch

Based on the Works of
L. Ron Hubbard

ISBN: 0-9661931-1-3

Registered with Library of Congress

WISE I/A # 03012601

Published by STI Publishing, a Division of Sales Technology
International, an enterprise of Lightening Productions. Printed in
the United States of America.

Creative direction by Nancy Fromer Frisch

Cover design and book layout by Rigney Graphics

SALES TECHNOLOGY INTERNATIONAL
STI Publishing
411 Cleveland Street, Suite 245
Clearwater, FL 33755
(888) 727-9992
(727) 466-6515
www.STIPublishing.com

This work is dedicated to

The Salesman

who has somehow miraculously managed
to keep commerce alive, armed only with
an odd assortment of hit-and-miss tools
and a persistent determination
to get the job done.

TABLE OF CONTENTS

SECTION THREE

FOREWORD

Whether you:

- Are considering becoming a salesperson,
- Have already begun a career in the field of sales,
- Are already a seasoned sales veteran, or
- Are just someone in need or want of some amazingly workable sales tools,

you are about to get a bright new look at a dusty old subject.

What you are about to read will sort out many inaccuracies and inconsistencies which you may have encountered and been confused by on the subject of sales.

The material in this book will acquaint you with the essential components of a sale in easy-to-understand ways that will enable you to creatively handle *any* sales situation you may ever encounter.

When you are done with this book, you will have all the basic selling tools a person needs to be a super success at the art of friendly persuasion.

SUPER SALESMANSHIP

HOW TO SELL – Clear and Simple introduces Super Salesmanship, the world's most effective win-win system of selling.

Super Salesmanship will show you how to develop your sale, step-by-step, in a way that will assure smooth and effective closes. It will show you how to persist and prevail through any and all resistance you may encounter during the sales process, and how to do it in ways that not only consistently close the sale, but actually enhance and strengthen, rather than weaken and harm, relationships with the customer.

Following the ultra-workable techniques of this five-step system allows a salesman* to:

- close his sales in high volume,

- leave his customers very well satisfied, and

- plant the seeds which, when properly nurtured, develop into referrals and repeat business.

By simultaneously satisfying the goals of the salesman, the customer and those of the business organization itself, Super Salesmanship stands alone at the pinnacle of workability.

Individuals who understand and effectively apply the principles of this five-step system will discover that they have gained the abilities to persuade virtually anyone on virtually any subject under virtually any legitimate circumstance, and are referred to in this book as "Super Salesmen."

---

* **NOTE:** From this point forward, the terms "sales*man*" and "sales*men*" refer to "sales*people*" and are not intended as an indication of gender. Additionally, "he" is used when referring to customers and potential customers for simplicity only.

A Special Note to the Non-Salesmen Among Us

> **The fundamentals of the art of "Sales" are one and the same as those of "Persuasion."**

So, even if you have no desire to have a career in sales, you will, by learning the theory and application of the techniques of the art of sales, become empowered to dramatically improve your personal and professional life in any and all sectors in which you DO wish to become more persuasive.

PREFACE

I want to share with you my prime purpose for writing this book.

Although I had been exposed to the world of sales from the time I was a little kid hanging around my family's retail clothing store in Port Chester, New York, I never thought of myself as a "salesman" during those early years.

After college, where I majored in the social sciences and did graduate work in the field of education, I tried my hand at several related careers. I did pretty well at them, but something always seemed to be missing.

And then I took a step that would forever change my life.

I discovered the works of the eminent American philosopher, writer and educator, L. Ron Hubbard. Hubbard's unparalleled understanding of communication and human nature, his life-changing educational techniques, and his ability to imbue his students with his own wisdom and masterful skills gave my life new vigor and direction.

At age 30, newly energized with an understanding of and a basic ability to apply Hubbard's principles of human interaction and communication—including key principles specifically addressed to the field of selling, I made a major career shift and reentered the sales arena . . . and the rest is history.

Applying Hubbard's principles, I became an instant sales phenomenon, winning awards, prizes, kudos and all of the great things super performance brings to one. And the most remarkable thing about my success was that, while consistently closing sales in high volume, *I was getting near-perfect Customer Satisfaction ratings,* as well as maintaining a steady stream of customers returning to make repeat purchases.

As the years went by, I came to realize that, to my knowledge, there had never been a book published on sales by anyone who was both an accomplished sales veteran and who had had the invaluable benefits of Hubbard's insights into the guiding principles of human interaction.

Having by now been in the field of sales for nearly half a century, having been recognized for my skills as a clear and easy-to-digest writer and as a highly effective educator, and having become a 25-year veteran in the application of Hubbard's ultra-workable principles of interpersonal relations, as well as being familiar with his key references directly on the art of selling, I found myself in a relatively unique position.

I decided that it fell onto my plate and was my joyful duty to pass along the understandings and skills that I had accumulated on the subject of selling, by writing this book.

• • • • •

The first principle that I ever became acquainted with of Hubbard's was one of the most powerful and useful principles of life itself.

It is a principle which underlays all of sales technology and permeates all the chapters of this book.

What one is trying to do, when selling, is to bring about *a mutual understanding*. One is trying to get the prospective customer to understand that he has a real need or want for the product, service or idea, and through the process of communication, to get him to agree to acquire it.

Hubbard discovered that *understanding* is itself made up of three definable components. And that these three components are directly interrelated to one another, like the three corners of a triangle. He discovered that to bring about an increase (or decrease) of understanding one need only increase (or decrease) any *one* of these three components.

The three components which comprise understanding are: *Affinity* (degree of liking), *Reality* (level of agreement) and *Communication*.

Simply stated: If one wishes to raise someone's willingness to communicate, he can do so by introducing more and more points of agreement into the conversation. If one wishes to raise someone's liking for a product, he can do so by getting that person into more and more communication with the product. If one wishes to get someone to agree to buy a particular product, service or idea, he can do so by building up their level of affinity and desire for that product. Raise any one of the three corners of the Affinity-Reality-Communication triangle and the other two corners will rise along with it.

In this book you are going to see the extraordinary power of some of the amazingly workable tools discovered by Hubbard–including this "ARC Triangle" (pronounced "Ay Are See Triangle").

• • • • •

My earlier sales book, HOW TO BE A SUPER SALESMAN . . . *and Still Respect Yourself in the Morning*, was greatly inspired by the works of L. Ron Hubbard.

I have been very gratified to receive so many testimonials and success stories from people whose careers and lives have changed for the better by applying the principles in that book.

In *HOW TO SELL – Clear and Simple*, I've taken it a notable step further by bringing the book into full alignment with the remarkable works of L. Ron Hubbard.

I believe you will find that these new additions better reveal the source of the book's strength and will forever change your ability to close sales, satisfy customers beyond expectation and build future business.

ACKNOWLEDGEMENTS

- To my mother, Leah Frisch, the very powerful and unique individual, businesswoman and artist, who gave me my early start in the world of sales.

- To my dear wife, Nancy Fromer Frisch, a world-class master of marketing, for being my steadfast friend and supporter, invaluable advisor, and talented editor throughout the development of this project. Without her continuous confidence in me and non-stop assistance with this project, this work would not have come about.

- To my bright and beautiful ten-year-old daughter, Daisy, for bringing so much sparkle into our lives.

- To those dear friends and colleagues who contributed their precious time, their valuable suggestions and their words of encouragement to help bring this product to fruition.

- To one of the world's truly great characters, my brilliant friend, Don Tolan, whose personal belief in me, and aggressive support of my earlier work, provided me valuable opportunities and my work meaningful exposure, without which this book might never have gone into development.

- And a very special thanks to L. Ron Hubbard for being the best friend the sales world has ever had.

*"The whole economic structure
needs the salesman; he is the
key of the whole structure."*[1]

—L. Ron Hubbard

INTRODUCTION

The entire world of commerce depends and pivots upon the performance and transactions of the salesman. As a result, sales is one of the highest paying of all professions.

So why is it, do you suppose, that when you suggest to someone that they become a salesperson, they often turn pale, break into a cold sweat, and frantically assure you that they just don't have what it takes?

Few fields are less well understood or more strewn with false beliefs than the field of sales.

Yet, just as in other professions, the actual ingredients that spell success in sales can be named, taught and mastered.

In this book, you are going to learn the fundamental essentials of Super Selling.

THE UNDERLYING ELEMENTS

The basic ingredients of a Super Salesman include:

- EFFECTIVE COMMUNICATION SKILLS;
- THE ABILITY TO FOSTER AGREEMENT;
- COMPETENCE TO SET AND THE FORTITUDE TO REACH GOALS;
- A CARING, HELPFUL, PROFESSIONAL AND ETHICAL ATTITUDE; and a
- WILLINGNESS AND ABILITY TO LEARN.

These elemental ingredients of good selling can be developed in and improved upon by almost anyone.

THE PROCESS HAS STEPS

A sale is made up of *five* distinct steps which follow one another in a particular sequence.

If you are new to the field of sales, you will learn precisely what these steps are, and why these five steps are in the exact sequence they are in.

FOR SEASONED PROFESSIONALS

For you veteran salesmen who are already acquainted with these steps to one degree or another, you'll discover that the sequence of these steps is being presented to you in a unique way—a way that will assist you to identify and polish your own winning techniques and bring a higher level of understanding and enhanced ability to control your sales.

With newly enhanced understanding of the individual steps and the sequence in which they come together, you'll be able to more creatively develop and more effectively correct any variation of sales situation in which you may find yourself.

Simply *knowing* more exactly what these five steps are and how they relate to one another should

INSTANTLY IMPROVE YOUR
ABILITY TO MAKE THE SALE.

HOW TO USE THIS BOOK

The main emphasis of this book will be to present you with a clear understanding of THE FIVE STEPS of a sale, and to firmly set you on the road toward becoming a confident master of this five-step process.

Super Summaries

At the end of each chapter is a Super Summary, designed to help you quickly and easily review the key points of that chapter.

Save What's Right, Change What's Wrong

As you read through this book, you'll recognize many things that you've been doing right and perhaps spot a thing or two that could use a bit of improvement.

I strongly suggest you keep a notebook handy. In one section of the book, develop a list of what you are already doing well. In a separate section, make a list of those areas you are interested in improving.

Use the "already doing well" items as your list of techniques which should be *preserved*. Review this list at the times when your sales are going especially well to validate and fortify your winning techniques. Also review the list when your sales are going especially badly to spot any earlier winning techniques that might have slipped away.

Each week or so, take an item from the list of "areas in need of improvement" and work on that area until you feel you've made noticeable improvement in it.

It is very helpful to copy the item you are going to work on that week onto an index card and keep the card handy.

Use the card:

- Just before beginning a sale to remind yourself of what principle you are working on; and

- Just after finishing with your prospect* to review how well you applied it.

The basic elements in this book, well learned and skillfully applied, can bring tremendous success to a salesperson. And when they are ethically as well as skillfully applied, they can bring an enduring sense of pride and satisfaction to the salesman, and an increased stability to the whole economic structure.

---

*Prospect: The person to whom you are trying to sell your product, service or idea.

SECTION ONE

> *"A fixed idea is something accepted without personal inspection or agreement."*
>
> *"It blocks the existence of any contrary observation."*[2]
>
> —L. Ron Hubbard

1

WHAT A SALE IS NOT

When I first started selling, I often found myself snarled up because I just didn't know what the real ingredients were that made up successful selling. And compounding my confusion were all of the faulty, fixed ideas about selling that sales managers and other more experienced salespeople around me held to be true and tried to push off on me.

Before launching into the essence of what it is that truly makes selling good selling, let's take a quick look at seven of the most widely held misconceptions about the field of selling. Left uninspected, these misconceptions can act as stumbling blocks, blinding us to the more workable truths, on the road to Super Salesmanship.

MYTH #1—Great Salesmen Are Born That Way

Super Selling requires the right combination of skills, attitudes and know-how.

Few humans are born with all these ingredients in place. While it might give one fellow a selling edge over another if he already has a silver tongue, a naturally smooth, pleasing manner, a charming sense of humor, an attractive appearance, etc., all this really means is that he might not have to work quite as hard for his sales success as the rest of us.

To become and remain a Super Salesman, you don't need to depend on being *born* that way. The most winning attitudes can be adopted, the right basic skills can be learned, and the know-how that makes it all look easy can be developed with experience.

So, whether you were born with an edge or not, to *assure* your success, your best bet is to adopt the winning attitudes, develop the right skills, and earn your know-how the old fashioned way, through practice, practice, and MORE practice!

MYTH #2—Most Salesmen Are "Pushy"

"Pushy" is also not an inherent personality trait that would show up on a DNA analysis of a salesman's genes.

While it is true that some salesmen *are* pushy, I believe you will discover that these are usually salespeople who are in need of more training and sharper skills.

It is a poorly skilled or inexperienced salesman who resorts to excessive PUSHING or PULLING of his prospect in an effort to shove or drag him forward in the sales process.

Persistence and "pushiness" are not the same concept. It has been my observation that the more skilled and experienced a salesperson truly is, the more he is able to LEAD his prospects, step-by-step, through the process of a sale, smoothly exerting just the right amount of force as he persists his way forward.

MYTH #3—The Mark of a Good Salesman Is His Ability to Speak Well

This principle would be more accurately stated as, "The mark of a good salesman is his ability to *communicate* well."

While the gift of gab truly can be a plus, and the willingness to outflow communication is essential, it is only part of the story. Good communication and good salesmanship also require the ability to *listen* well.

This particularly comes into play when the prospect is telling the salesman what his requirements are regarding the product or service in question.

The salesman who listens well to his prospect's specific needs and wants will be notably more effective in subsequently gaining the prospect's strong interest in his product or service.

MYTH #4—Control Is a Bad Thing

"Control," as a way of dealing with other people, has often had the dark connotation of being a sinister, self-serving method of manipulating others strictly for one's own gain. This is probably because it has sometimes been used in just that way. When *we* refer to control, however, in relationship to Super Selling, we are referring to it as a helpful tool being used in a good and caring way.

A proper sale is a process that takes a prospect, who is in need or want of something, through a series of steps, which results in the person acquiring that thing he needs or wants.

> *Control is the guiding force which makes certain that the prospect successfully gets through the process so that he does indeed end up with what he needs or wants.*

Sometimes the prospect is so motivated to acquire the desired item that it requires very little control from the salesman to move him though the steps of the sale (and a salesman should remain alert to this possibility so that he exerts no more force than is necessary). Often times, however, despite his need for the product or service, the prospect falls victim to his own sales resistance and may require a considerable amount of control to move him through the process. The salesman should always be alert to this possibility as well and be willing to exercise however much control it takes to get the prospect through the process. There are exact tools which allow a salesman to smoothly keep a dialogue going forward, despite the prospect's saying "No," that are neither "pushy" nor highly objectionable to the prospect.

In the following chapters, you will be given these tools—as well as a simple technique which will allow you to instantly take control back any time a prospect inappropriately attempts to take over.

MYTH #5—The Primary Purpose of "QUALIFYING"* a Prospect Is to Discover How Ready and Able He Is to Buy Your Product

Discovering how ready and able the prospect is to buy is useful information for the salesman in determining how much time and energy to put into trying to sell to a particular prospect. But trying to discover how ready and able the prospect is should be of *secondary* emphasis and come only AFTER you have demonstrated a significant amount of interest in understanding his personal needs and wants.

---

* Qualifying: Discovering relevant data about your prospective buyer.

In Super Salesmanship, the *primary* purpose of qualifying a prospect is NOT to discover how ready and able he is, but to learn what his *needs and wants* are in relationship to the product or service you are trying to sell to him.

This data of what his needs and wants are enables you to smartly select *which* of your products or services is the most appropriate for him. It also guides your decisions on exactly *how* you are going to unfold your product or service to him.

And perhaps just as importantly, your display of sincere interest in learning about your prospect and his personal preferences and requirements can go a long way in building his confidence in you as a trustworthy, caring person.

Trying to extract from him how ready and able he is to buy, before demonstrating your interest in him, can easily undermine his confidence in your intentions and, in the long run, undermine the success of your sale.

MYTH #6—The "CLOSE"* Is All that Really Counts

Many sales professionals put far too much attention on the *closing* of their sale and far too little on the opening and developing of it.

A smooth close is built upon a sequence of properly executed earlier steps. If you've thoroughly laid these earlier steps in place, then getting your prospect to close should NOT take a massive effort or require resorting to complex tricks.

If, on the other hand, you have totally omitted or partially neglected one or more of the earlier steps, and have thus built a

---

* The Close: Getting a firm commitment to buy, including any applicable paperwork fully completed and payment secured.

faulty foundation, you will most likely find your closes enormously strenuous and often nearly impossible to pull off.

MYTH #7—Salesmen Can't Be Trusted

This widely held opinion undoubtedly arises, at least in part, from unhappy experiences many of us have had from time to time with a salesman.

Perhaps he was not completely ethical, or maybe he was just not properly knowledgeable about his product or his field in general, and subsequently misled us into a poor decision.

Perhaps we paid more for something than we later found out it was worth.

Or perhaps we were sold a completely false bill of goods and ended up with a totally worthless product.

In any case, we ended up with the short end of the deal and that added one more confirmation to the case that salespeople are untrustworthy, lying snakes.

The truth is . . . some of them are!

A few reptiles can give the whole place a bad name

Most are not, but some salesmen *are* quite unethical. As in any profession, all eggs are not good ones. But as in any profession, it would be a mistake to condemn the entire group for the few rotten eggs who tarnish the group's reputation.

It has been my experience that the great majority of salespeople are, by far, service-oriented people of good will who sincerely strive to help their public acquire whatever they might need or want in a fair and upright manner.

You can feel proud to be a member of these ranks simply by conducting your own sales in ways which leave you feeling proud of yourself.

When the confusions of incorrect, unworkable ideas about selling are identified and set aside, the road to understanding the workable, winning principles of Super Salesmanship is greatly widened.

SUPER SUMMARY
Chapter One

- Selling is made up of a specific set of skills which nearly anyone can learn to apply effectively.

- The ability to smoothly *lead* your prospects through the process of a sale is developed through good training and practice.

- How attentively you are able to *listen* is as important as, if not more important than, how smoothly you are able to speak.
  - Proper listening demonstrates to your prospect that you care about and are interested in him.

- It is a winning practice to use whatever amount of control it actually takes to make sure your prospect acquires the product or service that he needs.

- Qualifying is the process of discovering your prospect's needs and wants *as well as* the process of discovering your prospect's readiness and ability to acquire your product or service.

- Trying to find out how ready and able your prospect is *before* demonstrating your interest in his needs and wants can easily undermine his confidence in you and in the sale.

- The earlier steps which lead to the close are the very foundation upon which the close is built.
  - The more thoroughly you understand and establish these earlier steps, the less strenuous effort you will need to exert on the close and the more over-all control you'll be able to maintain.

- While some salesmen *are* quite unethical (as are a minority in any profession), most are service-oriented people of good will, striving to do the right thing.

- You can be *proud* to be a salesman!

2

WHAT A SALE IS

Selling, when properly done, is the process of locating a likely prospect in need or want of a product, service or idea, and caringly bringing that prospect to the point where he buys that product, service or idea.

GETTING ON THE STICK

In sales, as in any other field, you become able to control the process only to the degree that you develop understanding of:

- The steps that make up the process, and

- The underlying principles upon which the process is based.

For example, if you only learned to drive on an automatic transmission, then the only type of vehicle you would be able to control is one with an automatic transmission.

If one day you found yourself behind the wheel of a car with a manual transmission, you would probably find yourself staring at a strange-looking stick and going nowhere.

On the other hand, if you learned the basics of an automobile from bottom up, including how to drive both versions of transmission, you'd be potentially capable of taking control of

ANY automobile,

at ANY time,

under ANY circumstances,

and making it take you

ANYwhere you wanted to go.

And so it is with learning how to sell.

THE WHOLE AND ITS PARTS

You need to understand the how-tos and the why-fors of the whole and all of its parts to truly stay in control of a sale under any and all circumstances.

Simply put, a sale is a process of steps which begins by finding someone to sell something to and ends with that person buying what you are trying to sell him.

Despite how uncertain and imprecise a process it might have *appeared* to be when you think back on sales you've tried to make or sales someone tried to make on you,

> ### *The process of a sale has FIVE specific, definable steps.*

Each of these steps, when executed effectively, lays the foundation upon which the next step can be securely built. The earlier steps should form the solid base upon which, ultimately, a smooth close can be developed, allowing the salesperson to get a firm commitment and make the sale.

THE FIVE STEPS OF A SALE

1) **PROSPECTING** – Locating a potential buyer

2) **OPENING** – Getting the prospect into communication

3) **QUALIFYING** – Discovering certain relevant data about the prospect

4) **PRESENTING** – Enlightening the prospect about the product, service or idea and interesting him in acquiring it

5) **CLOSING** – Getting the prospect's firm commitment to acquire the product or service, with all applicable paperwork signed and sealed and finances finalized

Why These Steps? And Why in This Order?

The structure of a sale is not what it is because someone says it is, nor for any other such arbitrary reason.

The sequence lines up as it does because THAT'S WHAT WORKS!

> ***Each subsequent step depends for its success on the earlier steps being in place.***

The *second* step of a sale has to have the *first* step in place in order for the second step to be properly and stably erected. The *third* step needs the *first and second* steps in place for that third step to properly occur. And so on all the way up to the fifth and final step, Closing, which needs ALL of the earlier steps in place to stably support it.

This *is* the sequence a sale would ordinarily need to follow in order to predictably do what it is supposed to do . . . result in a sale!

A VIEW FROM THE REAR

Somewhere along the way, I discovered that the easiest way to grasp the logic of this sequence is, believe it or not, to view the sequence *backwards!*

So, before we begin our examination of each of these steps in depth, let's take a quick backwards look at a sale, starting with where it *ends* (with a firmly committed prospect) and work our way back to where it begins (finding someone to sell something to).

The Process in Reverse:

Step 5—CLOSING

What you are ultimately striving for in the sales process is to make the sale, to "CLOSE" it, to get a firm commitment from the prospect. This would be his solid agreement, in writing where applicable, that he will acquire from you whatever product or service you have been offering to him, with monies fully in place.

Step 4—PRESENTING

However, before you can expect him to firmly commit to *acquiring* your product or service, your prospect would first need to somehow be introduced to it (to learn about it, be told about it, perhaps be shown it, maybe get to experience it). He would need to be "PRESENTED" it. And he would need to be presented it in such a way that he sees the value and benefit of it to him—a value and benefit at least equal to the price you are asking him to pay for it.

Step 3—QUALIFYING

Before you can *meaningfully* present how the features of your particular product will be of proper benefit and value to him specifically, you must first learn from him what it is about him and his needs and wants that this particular product might satisfy for him.

And similarly, before you can effectively strategize your campaign of exactly which of your wares to present and how soon and how intensively to present them to this particular prospect, you had better learn what his *readiness and ability* are to experience and acquire whatever it is that you are selling.

This discovering of his relevant needs, wants, readiness and ability is the "QUALIFYING" step.

Step 2—OPENING

Now, before you can hope to get your prospect to tell you anything about anything, you've got to first get him *willing to communicate* with you. And before you can get him to *truthfully* tell you about himself and about the needs, wants and limitations of his life, you've got to get him to at least have some basic trust in you. Establishing this communication with basic trust is the "OPENING" step.

Step 1—PROSPECTING

And before you can even begin to get anyone into *any* kind of communication with you at all, you first have to *locate him!*

Locating someone to sell something to is the "PROSPECT-ING" step, and where the sequence of your sale begins.

This might all seem so simple that it hardly needs to be stated. Well, truth is like that sometimes! It can be staring us right in the face, but until something or someone directs our attention onto it, we often just don't quite see it.

$$\bullet \ \bullet \ \bullet \ \bullet \ \bullet$$

As we move forward into this book and you deepen your understanding of each of these five steps and their relationship to one another, you should become more and more able to think with and be creative with the process of a sale.

You will find yourself becoming less and less dependent on having to "feel your way through" a sale, and more and more able to effectively control anything and everything that comes your way.

If this logic made sense to you, you are ready to move forward and take a harder look at the highly specialized tech of each of the five steps of a sale. (If not, I suggest you reread this "Process in Reverse" a time or two until it does make sense to you before moving forward.)

- You will be able to control the sales process to the degree you understand the process and its underlying principles.

- THE PROCESS OF A SALE HAS FIVE SPECIFIC, DEFINABLE STEPS:

  - Step 1—PROSPECTING—Locating someone to sell your product or service to.

  - Step 2—OPENING—Getting the prospect willing to communicate with you openly.

  - Step 3—QUALIFYING—Learning what *needs and wants* your prospect has that your product or service might satisfy for him, and how *ready and able* the prospect is to acquire that product or service.

  - Step 4—PRESENTING—Enlightening the prospect about and interesting him in your product or service.

  - Step 5—CLOSING—Getting a firm commitment from the prospect to acquire that product or service, with paperwork complete and finances fully in place.

- When you lay each of the earlier steps of the sequence in place, you are providing yourself the firm foundation upon which to build each of the subsequent steps.

SECTION TWO

The Five Steps of a Sale

3

STEP ONE: PROSPECTING

The first step in the sales sequence is to find someone to whom you might be able to sell something. Ideally, this prospective customer you locate is a highly qualified prospect, meaning he already has a strong demand for your product and a good ability to buy it.

But highly qualified or not, you must first locate someone to potentially sell something to before you can go any further with the sale.

Each mode of selling—such as retail, wholesale, door-to-door, telephone sales, etc.—will tend to have its own most workable systems for prospecting. But, one thing they all have in common is that

> ### *Prospecting is a numbers game.*

NARROW IT DOWN

Of the billions of people and millions of businesses out there in the world today, there are almost certainly a very large number of potential prospects, if not hot prospects, for your product, service or idea, no matter *what* it is you are offering for sale.

Be it by national television campaign or by a magnetic sign stuck to the outside of your car, how large a piece of this enormous potential you decide to go after is up to your ambitions and the size of your marketing budget.

The challenge is to work your way through whatever size piece of the population you decide to take on and keep narrowing that piece down, until you connect up with the prospects who already have or can be assisted to develop a demand for acquiring your product.

Flying Solo

You may have to do it all on your own, like the door-to-door or telephone canvasser, for example, who goes through a neighborhood, knocking on every door or dialing one number after the next, discovering if the person on the other side of the door or on the other end of the phone line might already have, or be a potential candidate to develop, interest in the product he is offering.

This "cold canvassing" is a somewhat broad, shotgun approach. You fire blindly at every doorbell or telephone number in front of you, and hope that one of the shots will connect you with an actual, viable prospect.

As difficult as many find it to brave this raw style of prospecting, it has been successfully done since the original inventor of the stone wheel hired the world's first salesman to unicycle his way from cave to cave, peddling this "great breakthrough."

In addition to yielding some degree of success, this canvassing style of prospecting furthermore guarantees to thicken the skin of anyone who is willing to persist at it long enough.

Even if you are only a "one-man show," there are some methods of prospecting that are more sophisticated than canvassing shotgun-style, which you may choose to pursue on your own or with the assistance of some good hired help.

Team Effort

If you are an independent salesperson, such as a real estate agent, and can afford it, you may decide to hire an assistant or an outside marketing company to help do some or all of your preliminary "narrowing-down" prospecting for you.

Or, if you are part of a large enough organization, your own Marketing Department will probably be doing some or all of this preliminary prospecting for you through advertising and other forms of sales promotion.

• • • • •

Prospecting can be as tough as the hit-and-miss techniques of the lonely door-to-door salesman, or it can be as easy as working on a showroom floor where almost everyone who walks in off the street has heard your company's name and seen your company's ads and has already developed a healthy demand for what you are selling.

But easy or hard, with help or without, unless you have access to a divining rod that lets you know exactly where your best prospects are hanging out, someone is going to have to start from scratch and reach out to begin the search for or development of your prospects. And in all cases, whether you do your own prospecting or not,

> *It is you, the salesperson, who is ultimately responsible for assuring yourself a steady supply of prospects.*

HOW DO YOU DO IT?

At the very heart of prospecting is effective communication which reaches out and directly or indirectly tells your potential prospects something about you, your products and/or your organization.

While it's true that certain techniques have, over time, proven more effective than others, the ways in which you can go about prospecting are limited only by the bounds of your imagination and what you can afford.

Here are a few of the broad techniques which are among the best of the proven winners:

SALES PROMOTION

Sales promotion can be generally defined as ALL communication, activities and events, which, along with advertising:

- Let potential prospects know about your products, your services and your organization; and

- Are intended to increase sales.

Several forms of sales promotion are:

- WORD-OF-MOUTH COMMUNICATION—Any one-on-one recommendation of a product or service. This is usually considered the most effective form of sales promotion.

- LIVE EVENTS COVERED BY THE MEDIA—Such as a remote radio broadcast from your place of business.

- POINT-OF-SALE—An attention-getting display where the product is being offered for sale, such as a chef demonstrating a set of specially priced pots and pans in the housewares section of a department store.

ADVERTISING

This is promotion which is done for a product or service on a *broad* basis, such as with:

- Radio
- TV
- Newspapers
- Magazines
- Direct Mail—An offer sent out by traditional mail or e-mail to a specific public (perhaps containing discount coupons or a reply form)
- Flyers
- On-line promotion—via your own website or ads on other, related sites

It is important to

Customize your message for and distribute it to your most likely prospects. And make it easy for the prospects to respond.

EXAMPLE:

You have 10,000 flyers delivered to all home owners in a particular neighborhood, offering free information on a program that can lower their mortgage rates. You include a toll-free number, a fax number and perhaps an e-mail address. Of the 10,000 recipients, perhaps 100 call, fax or e-mail to ask for more information. These 100 are now identified or *located* as prospects or "leads" for you or your sales force to contact directly.

Use Urgency

Urgency is a powerful ingredient to build into your sales promotion.

It's designed to attract potential prospects to *immediately* step forward, out of the general population, and reach into your place of business.

> ***You can create urgency by limiting either the TIME a prospect would have to respond or by limiting the AMOUNT of product available.***

Examples of this are the TV or newspaper ads which announce: "Available for a limited time only! . . . While supplies last! . . . A free trip to Hawaii with every new refrigerator delivered by month end!" etc.

Promote Regularly

A sure way to guarantee that you will successfully maintain a steady supply of prospects is to effectively advertise and otherwise promote on a regular basis. You need to *repeatedly* tell them about yourself and your product or service.

That way, when a potential prospect develops enough demand for your product or service, he will also have built up awareness of you and your product line and know what, where and from whom he should make his purchase.

Many of those who write in, call or come in in response to your advertisement may turn out to be not yet very *ready* or *able* to buy. Some may be of higher potential, *almost* ready and able to be developed into buyers in the near future. And some will likely turn out to be those ready and able buyers you've been hoping to connect up with.

Much could be, and has been, written on the vital importance of sales promotion and advertising. If you yourself don't feel you have the interest or expertise to do your own, get help from an expert in the field. The good ones can be worth their weight in gold.

NETWORKING

In networking, rather than concentrating on reaching into the general population for fresh contacts, you

> *Utilize your already established*
> *circle of contacts*

and attempt to sell your products or services directly to them and to *their* circle of contacts.

If your line of products is suitable for a wide, general public, such as vitamins or cosmetics, your friends, neighbors, family members, co-workers, etc., would all be likely prospects to whom you might try to introduce your line of products.

If, however, your products or services are more specialized, such as computer software for business applications, you would want to network more selectively, to those contacts who would be likely prospects for your products, such as business associates, professional organizations, fellow breakfast club members, etc.

> *View any and all new contacts you make*
> *as potential prospects.*

REFERRALS

Prospects you get through referrals are generally very high quality prospects. Working hard to get such referrals is almost always worth your while.

Networking for Referrals

Just as your circle of contacts may be a good source of direct sales, so may they also be a good source for referring additional prospects to you. You may wish to

> *Ask at every appropriate occasion,*
> *"Who do you know that might need*
> *or want this product or service?"*

Happy Customers Are Super Sources

An extremely effective way to prospect is to ask those happy customers who have already done business with you to refer others they know who might similarly benefit from such a service or product.

Tell Them Who Sent You

You can gain the inside track with such a referral simply by letting them know you come to them via the customer who referred you to them:

SALESMAN: ". . . Peter Dolan just upgraded the air purifica-
tion system at his Bar-and-Grill with one of our

models and thought that your nightclub might also benefit from one of our units. . . . "

Even better is if your customer lets his friend or associate know that you will be contacting them. It can give you built-in credibility.

Ask at the End

> ***An excellent time to ask for referrals is just following the conclusion of your sale.***

Your prospect is very likely to be at the pinnacle of excitement about his purchase right after concluding his deal or shortly after taking delivery of your product—and probably at the height of his willingness to recommend you and your product to others.

EXAMPLE:

CUSTOMER: "Well, thank you so very much for your help! I can't wait to start using my new camera."

SALESMAN: "You're most welcome. So Frank, let me ask you something. *Who else do you know who could use a good zoom?*"

CUSTOMER: "Timely question! Several of the members in my camera club are talking about upgrading and I'm sure they'd appreciate the level of service I've received from you."

SALESMAN: "Nice of you to say so. Would you be willing to arrange it with your club for me to give a presentation of the latest models at your next meeting?"

CUSTOMER: "No problem. I'll get it all set up and give you a call by next Tuesday."

No Sale—But YES, Referrals

You will, on occasion, have prospects who are very impressed with your product or service and pleased with the way you handled them, but for one reason or another, end up not buying your product from you.

Though they may not have given you the sale, they may still be more than willing to give you some referrals.

So, don't hesitate to ask them if they know of anyone else who might be in the market for your product(s). Their referrals can more than make up for the loss of *their* sale.

PROFESSIONAL REFERRALS

An excellent source of prospects is referrals from your fellow professionals. Once they are aware of your services and trust you, they may be willing to send you prospects who are likely candidates for what you are offering.

For example, managers of local, traditional clothing stores might send customers in need of a tuxedo to your tuxedo shoppe. Regular shoe stores might refer special cases to your orthopedic specialty shoe store. A printer might run into people needing some help designing a flyer and refer them to your advertising agency.

Backtrack Them Down

There's a simple formula to help you locate excellent professional referral sources:

1) Figure out the *richest potential sources* from which your prospects might likely be coming.

2) Then backtrack down those trails and make cordial contact and effective arrangements to get the prospects relayed forward to you personally by the people who are handling them earlier on those pipelines.

Some examples of backtracking for referral sources are:

• New car salesmen contacting nearby auto repair shops, casualty insurance agents, tow truck companies, etc., to have them refer owners of cars which have been recently damaged beyond repair.

• Mortgage loan brokers contacting real estate agents to have them refer their buyers who may be in need of financing.

• Medical specialists contacting general practitioners for referrals of patients who need treatment in their field of specialization.

When requesting such referrals, *be certain to establish yourself as reliable, trustworthy and as someone who will deliver an excellent product or service to their referrals.*

Be sure to supply these referral sources with some of your business cards to hand out—and perhaps to display on their counters.

Show Your Appreciation

> **Referral sources can be extremely valuable and much care should be taken to properly nurture them.**

Be certain to *express your gratitude adequately.* At a minimum, be sure to:

- THANK OR OTHERWISE ACKNOWLEDGE THEM by phone, note or in person.

Under certain circumstances these sources should also be rewarded with:

- A FINDER'S FEE or perhaps by returning the favor and

- REFERRING BUSINESS THEIR WAY.

- AN OCCASIONAL GIFT is sometimes appropriate to the person or to his staff who referred your prospect.

You can make a fun game of it with tins of popcorn, a block of movie tickets, gift certificates to a local restaurant, etc.

SAVE THOSE FILES

Another superb source of prospects is to "recycle" your previous clients.

Whether your company is ready to bring out a "better mousetrap" or it's just time for a routine maintenance call,

> **One of the richest sources of potential business is your own file of existing customers.**

Creating and maintaining a properly cross-indexed file and mailing list of customers with whom you've successfully done business is a very worthwhile project.

As discussed more in the upcoming chapter on "Repeat Business," maintaining regular communication with your customer, client or patient base will not only greatly enhance *their* loyalty to you, it will also give you the convenient opportunity to periodically ask them for additional referrals.

• • • • •

Which specific prospecting methods you choose for yourself will be monitored by:

- Exactly what kind of product or service you offer;
- How large a public you intend to reach;
- What size budget you are operating with; and
- Which methods you are comfortable with or willing to apply.

There are whole books written on the vast subject of how exactly to go about prospecting. You may wish to research one or more of these for additional suggestions.

THE NUMBERS GAME AND PERSISTING THROUGH IT

You often hear sales referred to as "a numbers game." This is a comment on the need to persist through one's unsuccessful sales experiences. No one makes every sale. No one gets 100% response to his promotions. Your only assurance of success is to

Prospect in quantity.

Every salesman has to work his way through the ones he *doesn't* make in order to reach the ones he *will* make.

A key part of your job as a salesperson is to continue to reach out rather than get discouraged while working your way through. Keep the letters, e-mails, faxes and phone calls flowing out, as well as keeping up with personal contacts.

When you do persist to outflow communication in volume, you inevitably do make that next good connection and do make that next sale. And when you do, your confidence, energy and optimistic viewpoint seem to return along with it.

Which Rainbow Holds the Pot of Gold?

You never know which one of the people you are contacting will turn out to be, or develop into, the viable prospect you've been searching for. So, when prospecting, it is vital to keep your best attitude in place for each and every contact you make.

On the Road to Super Salesmanship, the number of viable prospects you end up with will depend solely upon your ingenuity and the volume of communication you flow out in pursuit of those prospects.

Super Summary
Step One: Prospecting

- Always ensure yourself a steady supply of prospects.

- Utilize professional assistance when needed.

- Promote regularly.
  - Reach out to your potential public and *repeatedly* tell them about you, your product and your organization.

- ADVERTISING AND PROMOTION
  - Customize your message for and distribute to your most likely prospects.
  - Include an offer designed to elicit a response.
  - Make it easy for the prospect to respond.
  - Build in *urgency.*

- NETWORKING
  - Utilize your already established circle of contacts.
  - View any and all new contacts you make as potential prospects.
  - For general-use products, everyone you know is a potential prospect.

more. . .

- REFERRALS
  - Prospects gotten by referrals are generally very high quality and well worth working hard to obtain.
  - Care well for your active referral sources.
  - Ask customers for referrals at the end of the close.
  - Ask customers for referrals shortly after delivery.
  - Ask customers for referrals on follow-up contacts.
  - Network your circle of contacts for referrals.
  - Backtrack down rich prospect trails and arrange to get a healthy supply of prospects referred to you.

- EXISTING CUSTOMERS
  - Keep files on earlier buyers for future prospecting.
  - Keep in periodic communication with these earlier buyers for repeat business and referrals.

- PERSIST!—With each contact you make that bears no fruit, know that you are that much closer to reaching one that will.
  - Keep up your positive attitude.
  - Keep up your momentum.
  - Keep up the volume of your outflow.

4

STEP TWO: OPENING

Once you have successfully located someone to begin selling something to, making the Prospecting step complete, what do you do next?

Next you have to penetrate through any resistance the prospect might have to communicating with you, and get the prospect willing to talk to you.

This is the "breaking the ice" step, or the "warming him up" step, or more formally, the second step in the sales process—the *Opening* step.

But how do you *do* it? And how do you know when you've done it? And what should you *avoid* doing while you're doing it?

The definition of an "open" prospect is a prospect who is willing to communicate openly to his salesperson.

Very often a prospect will open up quite quickly, if not instantly, just from the magical spark of your opening communication to him:

SALESMAN: (with sincere smile, excellent eye contact, an air of professional confidence and his arm extended to shake hands) "Hi. My name is Jerry. Welcome to Hot Tubs of Pasadena."

PROSPECT: "Hi, Jerry." (instantly opened) "My name is Herb. Tell me something. Does this model come in redwood?"

At other times, the prospect will be resistant and take a longer time before he's willing to communicate openly to you:

PROSPECT: "I'm just looking today," or
"Call back another time," or
"I'll call you if I have any questions,"
    or the like.

In professional sales circles, you'll hear much advice on how to go about executing this Opening step. You'll be told that "the best way to break the ice is to *always* smile" or to "*always* shake their hand" or "*always* show enthusiasm" or "*always* call them by their name at every opportunity," etc., etc.

In truth, most of these "always . . ." techniques do have at least some merit and workability, but only to the degree that they demonstrate sincere care and interest. None of these techniques tend to be very effective in the absence of care and interest. And when you apply them only mechanically, they can just about make your prospect's skin crawl.

Have you ever had an intense-looking salesman with dollar signs flashing in his eyeballs pounce on you?

Does this "opening" sound a bit too familiar?

> "Hi there, pal! My name's Lance, what's yours? Melvin? Oh, that's a . . . um . . . nice name. So, Melvin, how ya doin' today? Can I help put ya into one of our most prof-itab—er, I mean, into one of our most attractive models today? Huh, Melvin? Check out this one over here, Melvin. It's a beauty, huh, Melvin? What d'ya say? Can ya afford this one? Huh, Melvin?"

Would that put *you* into open communication with your sales-man?

To gain long-term, stable success in opening your prospects, you need to have a good understanding of the purpose of this step.

The exact purpose of Opening is to

> ### *Get your prospect into open, trusting communication with you*

so that it is possible for you to effectively lead him through the remainder of the sales process.

THE SENIOR GUIDING PRINCIPLE

A common denominator of, and probably the *greatest single secret* of effective opening techniques, is that they demonstrate you, the salesperson, as a:

- **CARING**,
- **INTERESTED**,
- **SAFE** and
- **HELPFUL**

person.

One tends to *trust* and be willing to communicate with caring, interested, safe, helpful people.

EXAMPLES:

- "Hi, my name is Jan and I'm calling from the XYZ Group. If you have a few moments, I'd like to tell you about a very special offer we just made available . . ."

- "Hello. My name is Mike and I'd like to assist you this evening with your . . ."

- "Hi. My name is Andy. If you're not already being helped by someone, I'd like to be of service to you in any way that I can . . ."

Keep It Up

If you find that your prospect is requiring more to open than a pleasant introduction, no matter *what* you choose to say or do to try to open him, stick to the senior guiding principle and continue to

> **Display yourself as a person who is CARING, INTERESTED, SAFE and HELPFUL.**

KEY GUIDELINES

The following key guidelines should make Opening easier for you:

- Just before contacting your prospect, take a moment to decide that "Helping this prospect is my #1 concern."

- Have one or more standard greetings you find to be highly effective and comfortable.

- Carry yourself with an air of professional confidence.
- Do friendly things like:
    - Greet the prospect promptly and pleasantly;
    - Introduce yourself by name;
    - Offer a handshake whenever appropriate;
    - Smile sincerely (even over the phone, that comes through);
    - Welcome him to your place of business and offer a tour to help orient him or a refreshment to comfort him (if applicable);
    - Refer to him by name only as often as it seems appropriate and comfortable;
    - Remain as agreeable and supportive as you honestly can;
- Say true things which he would find helpful;
- Ask whatever questions seem appropriate that show your sincere interest in and concern for him:

EXAMPLES:

"Have you lived in this area long?"

"Did you get to enjoy all that sunshine last weekend?"

"Is this handsome group of folks your family?"

"Is anyone assisting you?"

"Can I offer you a tour of our facility?"

- Do not ask self-serving questions that prematurely probe for vital selling data;
- Give real help and advice;

- Help your prospect feel as good and right as you honestly can about what he says to you and about the business he may give to you;

  - If your prospect is difficult to open and is continuing to act standoffish or seems to be trying to push you away—LET HIM!

FIRST IMPRESSION

The first impression you make on your prospect can be of utmost importance. Nearly *any* prospect will open quickly and easily if properly approached.

Cut Him Some Slack

If your prospect does not open quickly and is instead stand-offish, saying, for example, that it is not a good time for you to be calling him or stopping by to see him, or that before talking to you he wants to "look around some more first," or is in some other way letting you know that he wants to be left alone, often your best bet is to . . .

LEAVE HIM ALONE!

You could offer him the opportunity to browse the space or look through some literature (or to send him some literature if you are working over the phone) and offer to make yourself available if he has any questions. Use this as an *opportunity* for him to observe you as the caring, helpful salesperson that you are. And then leave him alone.

EXAMPLE:

SALESMAN: "Has anyone been assisting you?"

PROSPECT: "No, but that's okay. I'd prefer to look around a bit before getting any help."

SALESMAN: "No problem. Is this your first time into our showroom?"

PROSPECT: "Yes, it is."

SALESMAN: "Well, welcome. My name is Alan. Please feel free to examine anything that interests you. If you develop any questions or need any help, please consider me at your service."

Try Again

You can always recontact him a short time later, once again demonstrating yourself as caring and helpful. You can do this as early as *immediately* after thoroughly acknowledging his request to be left alone—or as much later as seems appropriate.

EXAMPLES:

(In person)

SALESMAN: "Have you been developing any questions I can help you with?"

(Over the phone)

SALESMAN: "Hello, Mr. Wright. This is Marty King of King Properties—we spoke last week. Do you have a moment? . . . I wanted to let you know that mortgage rates have dropped and this could be an excellent opportunity for you to take a look at some homes."

To the degree you have demonstrated yourself as interested, helpful, safe and caring, you will be successful upon reapproaching your prospect—or him reapproaching you.

A Friendly Smile

If you can have a sincere smile on your face for the first moment of communication you have with your prospect, it can carry you a long, long way.

This can, of course, sometimes be challenging if you are having a bad day—or are generally nervous or anxious, as many salespeople are when approaching someone new.

And yet you will discover that you have the ability to create such a sincere smile if you will simply *decide* to do so just before delivering your opening communication.

Serious Schmerious

A good way to look at it is that

> **Although making the sale may be important to you, it doesn't have to be SERIOUS.**

If you can manage to get the situation to seem a little less serious and a lot more like "fun," you're going to find yourself a lot more relaxed, smiling a lot more of the time and probably making a lot more sales.

Professional Confidence

Once your prospect becomes willing to communicate with you, you are going to be leading him through the steps of the sale—eventually asking him to buy the product or service you will be recommending to him. He is going to have to depend upon your judgment every step of the way. The time to begin building his trust in your professional competence is right from the opening moment.

When you approach your prospect, be certain to do so with an underlying air of confidence. That confidence will communicate to your prospect that you have an understanding and command of your area, from which he might benefit.

Confidence builds with experience and success. While you are building up your experience and success, you can simply *create* that air of professional confidence with which to approach each and every prospect.

Don't Delay the Initial Greeting

It's not only what you say and how you say it that goes into forming the prospect's first impression of you, but also *WHEN* you say it.

Ignore-ance Is NOT Bliss

I hate being ignored. Don't you?

Going into a place of business and having no one greet or approach you for many minutes, or calling a business on the phone and having it ring off the hook before anyone answers and/or being interminably parked on hold, tends to irritate people.

Ignoring people does not generally predispose them to want to give you their business. It predisposes them to take their business *elsewhere.*

Acknowledge Their Presence

If a potential prospect comes into your place of business,

> ### *Greet the prospect as promptly as possible.*

If the phone rings,

> ***Answer the phone as quickly after
> the first ring as you can.***

If a prospect writes or faxes or e-mails you,

> ***Get a reply back to him promptly,***

ideally within one business day.

If, despite the best of efforts, your prospect has been caused to wait excessively:

- Get back to him as quickly as you can;
- Thank him for his patience; and
- Apologize for any inconvenience.

GIVE BEFORE YOU TRY TO TAKE

Be willing to extend yourself. Let your prospect see that you regard him highly enough to invest your time and energy in him.

> ***Be willing to give real help and advice
> to your prospect before trying to
> extract anything out of him.***

Before you can expect to win your prospect's *interest*, or have him willing to *communicate* with you openly, or allow you to *control* the direction the sale is going to take, it is in your best interest to make sure your prospect recognizes you as someone who intends to *help* him.

EXAMPLE:

SALESMAN: "Does the room seem a bit warm to you?"

PROSPECT: "Yes. It does seem a little on the warm side for me. But there's no need to bother about it."

SALESMAN: "It's no bother at all. Let me go see if I can get the thermostat adjusted down a touch. Can I bring you a cold soft drink or some ice water on my way back?"

What's in It for *ME?*

If you ignore the "senior guiding principle" (to display yourself as a person who is caring, interested, safe and helpful) and approach your prospect with your attention primarily focused on what's in it for *you*, the prospect is likely to pick up on such a self-serving intention—and you will have built yourself a very steep road to climb.

How many times have you had a salesman start out by asking you questions like the following, designed to discover if you were just going to be a waste of *his* time?

- "How much down payment can you afford?"
- "How's your credit?"
- "Are you already committed to another salesman?"
- "Are you prepared to buy today if I show you what you want?"

All Questions in Their Right Time

As a salesman, you *will* need to know the answer to all of these sort of questions before the sale is over and done with.

But that will come LATER—*after* you've invested a proper amount of time and effort in your prospect—and well after the prospect is open.

Bum Data

If you try to push the sales process forward with probing questions *before* your prospect trusts you sufficiently to communicate openly to you, you risk the reliability of any data you subsequently get from that prospect. You risk that the subsequent data he supplies you with is "bum data"—a defensive smoke screen of half-true and untrue information which will eventually lead the two of you, NOT into the successfully completed sale you were hoping for, but rather into the misery and frustration of a NO-SALE dead end.

You'll find that those salesmen who complain that "buyers are liars" likely need to work some more on their opening techniques.

Richard's Cure-All

I once had a sales manager who handled any sales slump any of us ever got into the same way every time. He'd remind us that first and foremost a salesman's attention should be on *helping* the prospect in front of him. He'd say, "Forget about making a commission, or whatever you're thinking about. Go out there and only think about helping your next prospect and everything will go better."

And by golly . . . he was right! Everything would go better!

GIVE ME A SIGN

Some excellent indicators that your prospect is open are when he begins to:

- Tell you about what it is that he needs and wants;
- Ask you questions about your product or service; or
- Ask you for help.

EXAMPLES:

- "You know, what I could use is one of these round ones, but in a darker color."
- "Does your nutritional program help people lose weight?"
- "If you aren't too busy right now, I have a few questions about your upcoming spring product line."

• • • • •

YOUR WINNING STYLE

The techniques with which you choose to open your prospects need be limited only by their degree of workability and your good sense.

So long as you demonstrate yourself to be the CARING, INTERESTED, SAFE and HELPFUL person that you are, you should find little resistance and lots of satisfaction getting your prospects into open communication with you on your road to Super Salesmanship.

SUPER SUMMARY
Step Two: Opening

- Get your prospect to communicate openly with you.

- THE SENIOR GUIDING PRINCIPLE: Demonstrate yourself as the CARING, INTERESTED, SAFE, and HELPFUL person that you are.

- Just before contacting your prospect, decide that "Helping this prospect is my #1 concern."

- Carry yourself with an air of professional confidence.

- ALWAYS GIVE IT YOUR BEST SHOT AND MANY WILL OPEN INSTANTLY.
  - Have a sincere, friendly smile in place before you begin.
  - Be *determined*, not *serious*.
  - Have some standard greetings you find effective and comfortable.
  - Greet your prospect as promptly as possible.
    - Answer the phone as quickly after the first ring as you can.
    - Answer all correspondence promptly.
  - Introduce yourself by name.

- Offer a handshake, whenever appropriate.

- IF YOUR PROSPECT DOESN'T OPEN INSTANTLY:
  - Continue to demonstrate yourself as a caring and helpful person.
  - If he wishes to withdraw . . . LET HIM!!!—then,
    - Check back with him at the first chance you can appropriately create.
  - Be willing to invest some time and energy in your prospect.
  - Give before you try to take.
    - Make observations and ask questions that show your sincere interest and concern.
    - Don't ask premature, "What's in it for me?" questions.
  - Say true things that he will find helpful.
  - Refer to him by name only as often as seems comfortable and appropriate.
  - Remain as agreeable and supportive as you honestly can.

  - Help your prospect feel as good and right as you sincerely can about what he says to you and about the business he may give to you.

more. . .

- Your prospect is open when he is willing to honestly talk to you about his needs, wants and limitations.

- Discover and refine comfortable openings that work for you.

"In order to get response you've got to first find out what people want. You've got to find out what people consider valuable. When you know what people want and what they consider valuable, you know what they will respond to."[7]

—L. Ron Hubbard

5

STEP THREE: QUALIFYING

(OR "DISCOVERING")

Once the salesperson has successfully gotten his prospect to openly talk to him, what does he do next?

Let's take another look at this thing *backwards* for a moment:

As a salesman, you want your prospect to buy a product from you. But so far, you haven't *presented* one to him. You want to present one to him, but you haven't yet found out what it is about your product or service that he might consider desirable and of value.

So . . . the next thing you had better do is:

> *Find out enough data about your prospect,*
> *his needs, wants and limitations, to be able*
> *to design a presentation of your product,*
> *service or idea that will be meaningful*
> *and relevant to that particular prospect.*

This step of discovering relevant data about your prospect is commonly called Qualifying.

AT THE HEART OF IT ALL

Qualifying is at the heart of a sale. Without effective qualifying, a salesman will often be barking up a wrong tree. With effective qualifying, a salesman will find his success ratio rising notably.

How often have you had a salesman waste your time trying to sell you something that you neither *wanted* nor *needed*?

A salesman should find out that his prospect loves wool but hates polyester before spending too much of the prospect's time (and his own) trying to interest him in "The Suit of the Month"—which only comes in polyester.

Likewise, before telling his potential recruit all about the exciting possibilities of a multi-level marketing game, in which he must hold weekly meetings for hundreds, it would be a big timesaver (for both of them) for the salesman to discover that his prospect has a deathly fear of public speaking and no interest in overcoming it.

Attempting to present your product to your prospect or get him to commit to buying it, *before* understanding his needs, wants and limitations, is a sure formula for aggravating a lot of prospects and missing out on a lot of otherwise makeable sales.

In this Qualifying step you will be discovering:

- What your prospect's *needs and wants* are which your product or service will offer to satisfy;

- Those properties or characteristics of a product or service which he considers *unnecessary or undesirable* and would prefer to avoid; and lastly,

- How *ready and able* your prospect is to acquire your product or service.

It can also be very fruitful to take note of any other unique information that the prospect shares with you about himself and his circumstances, as it can help you to make the upcoming presentation of your product that much more personal.

WHAT ARE YOUR PROSPECT'S NEEDS AND WANTS?

The *prime* purpose of Qualifying is the ongoing process of learning enough data about a prospect's needs and wants in relationship to your product or service to make the balance of the sale highly relevant to that particular prospect.

Your prospect will value your product or service, and wish to acquire it, to the degree that he believes it has features that align with his wants and will satisfy his needs.

HOW DO I DO IT?

To be a Super Salesperson you need to

Demonstrate an attitude of interest

in your prospect and in the successful fulfillment of his personal or professional goals in relation to your product or service.

Ask Interested Questions

This attitude of interest should permeate the Qualifying step. The questions you ask should demonstrate your interest and should be primarily directed toward gaining an understanding of your prospect's requirements, preferences and limitations.

In this step, you need to be *interested,* not *interesting.* You will have your opportunity to be as interesting and entertaining as you can be in your upcoming presentation, but while qualifying, your job is to be *interested.*

EXAMPLE OF INTERESTING:

PROSPECT: "I prefer red."

SALESMAN: "Oh, yes. *My* whole family prefers red. My wife loves bright red. I, on the other hand, find reddish orange my personal favorite. Each of my children has his own shade of preference. My youngest . . ."

EXAMPLE OF INTERESTED:

PROSPECT: "I prefer red."

SALESMAN: "Oh, yes. Red is wonderful. Which shade of red do *you* find most attractive?"

Ask him questions which will let you

> ***Get acquainted with his priorities***
> ***in relationship to the product or service***
> ***you will be presenting to him.***

You should ask him any and all penetrating questions you can think of that will give you enough information about his requirements and limitations to enable you, in your upcoming presentation, to:

1) Smartly select which of your products or services is best for him, and then

2) Present how particular *features* of that product or service will *benefit* him by fulfilling his specific needs and wants.

Ask Open-Ended Questions

It's a big effort-saver to phrase your questions in ways which will encourage your prospect to flesh out his answers rather than simply answer "Yes" or "No":

- "What are the most important things to you in a new home?"

- "How do you mainly expect to be using the generator?"

- "In what ways were you hoping our service would improve your life?"

- "What qualities of your last set of clubs did you like the most?"

- "What things about your last phone system did you like the least?"

Listen Carefully

You had better listen *very* carefully to what your prospect tells you, because you are going to be using the data you discover here to customize your upcoming presentation of your product to this particular prospect's requirements. Always be thinking a bit ahead to your presentation. And unless you have a photographic memory, don't hesitate to take notes of your prospect's answers.

To the degree that you are successful in customizing your upcoming presentation to align with the data he just gave you,

you will be demonstrating your level of care, interest and competence:

> SALESMAN: "This refrigerator comes in almond cream, *which I believe you mentioned would match your stove.*"

To the degree that your upcoming presentation is *out of alignment* with the data he gave you, you will jeopardize his confidence in you and your abilities:

> SALESMAN: "So let me show you this great refrigerator, which is available in our newest color— AVOCADO GREEN!"

> PROSPECT: "Excuse me, Mr. So-called Salesperson. Where were you when *I mentioned I HATE avocado green?!*"

Reinforce His Preferences

How you respond to your prospect's communications to you on each of the preferences he confides in you can be of vital importance in shaping the direction the sale will take.

Each time he discloses a preference, such as:

"I like the dramatic effect of direct spotlight type lighting," or

"I'd rather not have the expense of adding more memory,"

acknowledge his preference in as agreeable and supportive a manner as you honestly can. And, so long as his preference is not one that is likely to later get in the way of the sale (such as for a color that is no longer available), let him know one or more things that you honestly believe are RIGHT about his preference:

"Well, sure. Direct lighting is stronger and more dramatic."

"Yes. From what you've already told me, I believe your needs would be met without any additional memory and that will save you some money."

Giving such agreeable, supportive assurances will reinforce your prospect's level of certainty that he is making the right decision. The more comfortable and certain he is with his decision, the more likely it is that he will feel secure enough to commit to the purchase when the time comes.

Be the Expert

There will also be occasions when it will serve your prospect and the situation better to *not* fortify, but rather to dissuade your prospect from his preferences.

For example, if you know that direct spotlighting would be a poor illumination source for the particular location; or if you are pretty certain that it would be a more optimum long-term solution for your prospect to go ahead and get the computer *with* the extended memory feature.

These may be decisions which you, as the more knowledgeable "expert," are more capable of making than is your prospect. While you never want to be any more disagreeable than is necessary, it is vital to your long-term peace of mind as a sales professional to

> *See to it that your prospects make winning choices, especially on the important decisions.*

At these times, be sure to acknowledge with understanding, as usual, but do *not* reinforce the preference. Try instead to guide your prospect toward the most optimum decision:

SALESMAN: "I understand your preference for direct spot-lighting. And all things being equal, such bright, direct lighting can create a nice dramatic effect. But *for your purposes*, I'm going to suggest indirect fluorescent lighting because you'll get a much cooler, non-glaring effect, which, as you mentioned earlier, is *your most important objective* in the work space."

Get It All

Ask no fewer questions than it takes for you to be confident you have penetrated deeply enough to have discovered all of the important things your prospect needs and is hoping for:

SALESMAN: "Now that we have narrowed down the size and color, what else, if anything, would you say is important to you in selecting a new fridge?"

PROSPECT: "Well . . . Convenience of use is definitely important to me."

Don't be afraid of asking too many questions here. That is rarely a mistake you can suffer from. Asking these questions demonstrates your interest in your prospect. Asking too *few* questions, on the other hand, is probably the most common mistake salesmen make—and one of the most costly.

THE KEY MOTIVATION

The Key Motivation is your prospect's main, core, single most important reason for needing and/or wanting your product. It's the underlying problem, to which your product or service would be the solution.

So long as your product has more significance than a pack of chewing gum, it is of very special consequence that you

> **Discover and take particular note of your prospect's KEY REASON for needing and/or wanting your product or service.**

EXAMPLE:

SALESMAN: "Of all the reasons you are in the market for a new refrigerator—what would you say is the single *most* important one to you?"

PROSPECT: "That's easy. I can never find anything in my old refrigerator. It's the most *inconvenient* refrigerator ever invented. It's like a black hole. Once you put something in there, it's never seen again. It's got solid shelves that I can't see through and *it drives me nuts whenever I'm hungry and short of time to have to dig around through those miserable shelves to try and find whatever I'm looking for.*" (His Key Motivation)

Once you understand what your prospect's main motivation is for having interest in acquiring your product, *you will know what it is about your product's features that this particular prospect would find most valuable,* giving you very powerful material with which to build a meaningful presentation and a mighty strong close.

EXPLORE THE ANSWER

Sometimes the prospect's answers need one or more follow-up questions to get the data clarified enough for you to take action:

PROSPECT:	"Well . . . I'd have to say that shelves I can see through is the only other really important thing to me."
SALESMAN:	"Do you prefer clear glass or wire rack shelves?"
PROSPECT:	"Oh . . . I hadn't thought about that. I guess the clear glass is what I'd need. Glass would be much easier to keep clean."
SALESMAN:	"I know exactly what you mean. Please step over here. I think we have JUST the model you are looking for."

NOT-WANTEDS

As you go along, you should also be taking note of those things that would be offensive to your prospect or that he simply considers he doesn't wish to have, or can't have, as a characteristic of the product or service he is seeking.

As you discover these "unwanteds," you should be getting a feel for *how* unwanted they are and *you should be thinking ahead to your presentation.* As we will be covering more in the upcoming chapters, you will either need to present only products that avoid such characteristics or, if you choose to present a product which contains one or more of these unwanted characteristics, you may need to deal with your prospect's concerns to help him overcome his considerations.

For example, if he has made it clear that he prefers a "quiet" product, you would try to avoid offering him a product that has excessive noise, or if all your products are noisy, you may, if his objection is strong, have to either outweigh his concern by showing him so much that is right about your product, or get into communication with him on the underlying problem he has with noise and try to help him overcome that consideration.

It is far better to become aware of what your prospect's dislikes are and how strong they are *before* spending both your time and his trying to interest him in a product or service that has the unwanted characteristics which could ultimately dead-end your presentation.

PREPARE A LIST

If you are being highly successful in your sales and you find that the qualifying questions you ask your prospects are mostly the same from one prospect to the next, you might wish to prepare a list of those common questions as a form and make up a supply of copies.

You could use the form as a checklist to interview each prospect during your qualifying. It would serve as an automatic reminder to make sure you are not skipping questions which would have been important to have asked.

It would also provide a good record of your prospect's answers for you to refer back to later, should you need to.

EXPECTATIONS

Meeting and exceeding one's customers' expectations is one of the great secrets of long-term success. Up ahead, in Chapter 8, "Follow-Through," we'll take a closer look at why this is so.

In order to help ensure that you will be meeting or exceeding your prospect's expectations, you will, of course, need to gain an awareness of what his expectations are.

If this is a situation in which the prospect has initiated the contact (in which case you would assume he has some sort of goals and expectations in mind for contacting you), and if your prospect hasn't made it perfectly clear to you by this point what exactly is the minimum he is hoping to get accomplished with you, be certain to ask him.

EXAMPLE:

SALESMAN: "So, Bob, let me ask you another question: What exactly were you hoping we could get accomplished for you today?"

PROSPECT: "I'm hoping you can help me find the exact model that would best fill my company's needs and write a proposal that I can take with me, for the purchase of the first thousand units."

EXAMPLE:

MEDICAL ASSISTANT: "What exactly were you hoping the doctor would be able to do for you today?"

PATIENT: "Well, I'm hoping he can relieve enough pain today so I can go back to work and then hopefully come up with some treatments to get me permanently fixed-up and functioning the way I was before the accident."

EXAMPLE:

SALESMAN: "Ideally, what would you like to get accomplished today?"

PROSPECT: "I'm really in the early phase of shopping, so if you can just show me what you have and not give me a hard time if I don't buy today, I'd appreciate it."

SALESMAN: "No problem. I'll show you what we've got and we'll just see how interested you are in it when we're done. How does that sound?"

PROSPECT: "Sounds great."

Unreal Expectations

If you discover that your prospect's expectations are too unreal to be met, let alone exceeded, it is most often best to get him to adjust those expectations as soon as possible once you've established open, trusting communication with him. Otherwise you run the very real risk of doing a fine job and still being left with a disappointed prospect.

EXAMPLE:

SALESMAN: "So, let me ask you another question, Bob: What exactly were you hoping we could get accomplished for you today?"

PROSPECT: "Show me a brand new, loaded, Sports Utility Vehicle that you can sell me for no-money-down with payments under $100-a-month."

SALESMAN: "Boy, I wish there were a way that I, or *anybody*, could do that for you. I'd grab one of those deals myself. How about if I help you find a model you'll be real happy with and then figure out a way we can get you into it as painlessly as possible?"

PROSPECT: "Sounds like a plan. Let's do it."

EXAMPLE:

DOCTOR: "Nice to meet you, Mr. Smith. What exactly were you hoping I'd be able to do for you today?"

PATIENT: "Well, Doctor Rick, I'm expecting that you'll get rid of all this here pain so I won't have to use medication anymore and get me all fixed-up back the way I was before the train hit me."

DOCTOR: "I certainly understand your hope and I truly wish I, or *any* doctor, could promise to do that for you in a single visit. And truthfully, on occasion, such a miracle does occur. But, what do you say we set our sights for today on reducing your pain and getting you back to work and then come up with a treatment plan designed to get you back to the maximum functionality possible?"

PATIENT: "Yeah. Getting me out of pain sounds great. Let's get me out of pain and back to work and then figure out the rest from there."

Once you know what your prospect's expectations are—how high he has set the bar—you know what you will need to do to meet or exceed those expectations. And for those times you discover his expectations are out of the realm of the possible, get him to adjust them down to where, with a super effort from his Super Salesman, his expectations are at a level that can be met or exceeded.

• • • • •

READY AND ABLE

In addition to finding out the prospect's needs, wants and not-wants, *Qualifying is also the step in which you discover how ready and able your prospect is to make a purchase.*

"Ready" has to do with how intense his interest, willingness and motivation are.

"Able" has to do with how *limited or unlimited* his financial situation is, his authorization to make the commitment on his own—and anything else that might limit his ability to acquire your product.

Taking the Prospect's Temperature

In sales language, how ready the prospect is or isn't is commonly referred to as how "hot" or "cold" a prospect he is.

The hotter the prospect, the more ready he is to committing to and executing the sale.

As a salesperson, you need to know how ready and able any particular prospect is in order to appropriately plan the optimum amount of time to invest and the intensity of effort to apply.

It would be a good idea, for example, before asking a very ready-and-able prospect to stand by and be patient while you roll out a super-deluxe presentation of your finest luxury automobile to a second prospect, to discover that this second prospect is currently between jobs, has just filed for bankruptcy and has no intention of actually making a vehicle purchase for the next eight years—at which time, he intends to buy a motorized scooter. (On top of which, he's actually just killing time while his wife cashes in food stamps for a six-pack at the market next door.)

A prospect who is ready and able to purchase "today" would usually merit more of your immediate attention and energy than one who is unable and/or unready to make his purchase.

Don't Pre-Judge

By the same token, you don't want to *prematurely* disqualify someone who only *appears* to not be sufficiently ready or able to merit your immediate and intense attention.

He Doesn't "*Look*" Like a Buyer

Sometimes a person appears as if he wouldn't be able to make the purchase by the way he is dressed or the manner in which he conducts himself, or perhaps by his age or the kind of car he drove up in.

It's not that you shouldn't take each of these individual pieces of data into account along with the data the prospect himself supplies to you. It's just that to *leap* to the conclusion that someone is not qualified simply based on their appearance is a losing policy that will cost you a lot of sales.

A 12-year-old newspaper delivery boy used to linger in our stereo shop, dreaming about "someday" owning one of our premium sound systems. All the salesmen but me dismissed him as a distraction.

Sometimes, when traffic allowed, I'd turn on some of his favorite equipment and let him listen to a few of his favorite tunes. Occasionally we'd chat about the merits of one component over another.

One evening, he came in and handed me a $700 pile of very hard-earned money and bought himself the system of his dreams. That night, as I stacked up the multiple boxes in preparation for the delivery, the rest of our sales force looked on with a whole new understanding of what it means to not prematurely disqualify a prospect based on his appearance.

How Much More Ready Can He Be?

Sometimes you will have a prospect who is more ready and/or able than he appears to be or is letting on. And other times you will be working with a prospect who truly considers himself to not be ready and/or able, but who, with a dynamite presentation and effective closing procedure, could be assisted by you to become ready and able.

It is always a winning attitude to

> ***Approach your prospect's readiness and ability to buy from the viewpoint, "How much more ready and able could I help him become?"***

You know you are applying this principle well when, after closing your sale, you at least occasionally hear the comment, "You know, I really had no intention of buying today."

Determination and Readiness

A wild variable in calculating how hot a prospect you are dealing with comes under the subject of how *motivated* he is to acquire your product. It is important to remember that

> ***A highly motivated prospect can create miracles.***

A prospect who has an intense yearning for what you are selling, but just can't afford it (or has some other apparently insurmountable barrier(s) standing in the way of his purchase), may truly surprise you by demonstrating an unexpected ability to overcome all barriers and buy your product. It's astonishing how quickly the money and other solutions can be made to appear and the acquisition take place.

Giving a motivated prospect the benefit of the doubt and going ahead and working with him, despite the apparency that he is not able to make the purchase, can many times end up being quite satisfying as well as financially rewarding.

EXAMPLE:

PROSPECT: "I really love these products, and can't wait to buy one, but right now I'm just shopping, because it will be a while before I have a good down payment."

SALESMAN: "I understand. But let's go ahead anyway and figure out which model would best serve your needs. Once we've zeroed in on that, we can worry about how to come up with a down payment."

The Moral of the Story

Don't lose out on sales by giving only half-hearted efforts to prospects who *appear* unready or unable to buy, when a good, thorough effort might easily reveal these prospects as, or transform them into, fully ready and able buyers.

CARING BUILDS TRUST

Good qualifying serves another enormously powerful function, above and beyond giving you the key needed-and-wanted and ready-and-able data about your prospect.

When your prospect experiences that you care enough about him to be taking up your valuable time being interested in and trying to understand his unique needs and wants, his *confidence and trust* in you and your selling procedure tend to increase.

A Note of Caution

Although it may be vital data for a salesperson to discover how ready and able a prospect is to buy, let me, at this point, repeat an important warning. Premature pumping of your prospect for this "ready and able" data by asking such blatant questions as:

- "You ready to buy today?"
- "Your credit any good?"
- "Can you get your hands on the down payment tonight?"

can be dangerous.

Probing for ready-and-able data too early in the sales process can give your prospect the impression that you are too interested in what's in it for you and too little interested in what's in it for *him!*

There is a time and a place for everything, and the time to ask blatant ready-and-able questions is *AFTER* you've attentively asked enough needed-and-wanted questions to clearly display your care and interest in your prospect.

Establish Credibility

If, in your upcoming presentation, you are going to claim that *the features of your product or service are the solutions to your prospect's problems*, you had better give that prospect sufficient opportunity to share what he would consider the vital details of his problem, before you present your product as his solution.

This factor is so true and so important to the smooth success of a sale that I will sometimes spend *extra* time allowing my prospects to detail out their needs and wants (beyond what *I* consider I actually must know to proceed into my presentation) just to have them rest assured that I really do understand their exact situation.

• • • • •

It is this combination of:

- Accumulating knowledge about your prospects' unique needs, wants and limitations; and
- Building their confidence and trust in you and your motives

that will be the firm foundation upon which you can construct an effective presentation.

And it is these *same* factors of:

- Knowledge of what importances your product might have to your prospect; and
- Build-up of trust in you personally

which will help you later, during "the close," to get the prospect over any barriers that may surface, which would otherwise have kept him from buying your product.

CREATING A DEMAND

There are times that you are more aware of your prospect's needs for your product than he is.

Ask Questions that Raise Awareness

As you learn more and more about your prospect and his needs and wants, you may spot features of your product or service which would be of value to your prospect in ways that he himself has not yet become keenly aware of.

Some of your qualifying questions can be used to help make your prospect more aware of needs he may have for your product:

SALESMAN: *"Would you like to consider power windows as one of the options?"*

PROSPECT: "I didn't have power windows in any of my other cars and I don't think I need them now."

SALESMAN: "No problem. The reason I brought it up was because you had mentioned that you've never owned a four-door sedan before. So, I wondered: *Might you want to consider power windows in order to have easy control of the windows in the rear?"*

PROSPECT: "Good point. Hadn't thought of that. Yes. Please show me a sedan with power windows."

The Cold Call Qualification

There are also times when your prospect has not yet become *at all* aware of his need for your product and may not yet have begun to develop *any* want for it, at the point you first get into communication with him.

EXAMPLES:

NEED: If unaware that his teeth are developing plaque, a prospect will be unaware that he needs something in his toothpaste to dissolve it.

WANT: Until mass mania made us aware of high platform shoes, the enchanted bra and Billy the Singing Fish, we hadn't yet developed that "gotta have one" desire for them.

In certain sales situations, such as telephone or door-to-door canvassing, your potential prospect is likely to have no prior awareness of the product you are about to offer him and therefore no awareness that he needs or wants it.

In such cases, once the prospect is open, before you would be able to proceed any further with effectively selling him your product, you would need to, as the first part of your qualifying step,

> ## *Help him become aware of his*
> ## *need or want for your product.*

For example, if you were going door-to-door, selling a book of coupons good for discounts at the neighborhood businesses, once you had completed your Prospecting step (someone has replied to your knock and opened the door) and completed your Opening step (your warm, friendly smile and non-intimidating voice have brought a receptive smile and open attitude), you then would be ready to go into your Qualifying step.

In cases like this, you would be aware of the prospect's probable need or want for your product (the savings he could enjoy at his local butcher, baker, candlestick maker . . . and dry cleaner) *before* your prospect was.

So, the next thing you would want to do is help make him aware of his need or want for your product by asking him some well-chosen, key questions:

SALESMAN: "Hi, there. My name is Guy."

PROSPECT: "Hi, Guy. You look like a trustworthy person I'd be willing to talk to. What can I do for you?"

SALESMAN: "Well, Sir, are you aware that a group of your local business professionals, many of whom you probably already do business with, have gotten together to make available to you and your neighbors the opportunity to enjoy several hundred dollars' worth of savings?"

PROSPECT: "No, I wasn't. But I'm interested. Please tell me more."

Your prospect now has a need or want developing.

SALESMAN: "Well, sir, do you ever get more than $5 worth of dry cleaning done at one time? Or $15 worth of automobile maintenance? Or do you ever do more than $20 worth of grocery shopping at one time?"

PROSPECT: "Yes. Quite frequently."

SALESMAN: "Great. Then, do you think you might be interested in saving 10 to 50% off the cost of these items when you next are in need of them?"

PROSPECT: "You bet."

You now have your prospect's awareness of his needs and wants for your product developed enough for you to effectively continue forward with your sales process.

ADAPT AS NEEDED

Qualifying is an ongoing process. The deeper you develop your relationship with your prospect, the more additional relevant data is apt to surface.

As you continue to develop the presentation and close of your sale, and continue to demonstrate your care, interest and helpfulness, your prospect's willingness to entrust you with increasingly sensitive information (or data they just hadn't thought of earlier) can also be expected to deepen.

So, be willing and prepared to modify your presentation and your close according to any new, relevant data which surfaces:

PROSPECT: "You know, Charles, I hope you don't think me too vain, but I believe I would be happier if we switched to a gold one because gold goes better with my hair color."

SALESMAN: "No problem whatsoever. If we don't have a gold one in stock, we'll special order one right away and have it for you in no time at all."

• • • • •

IN CONCLUSION

Discovering your prospect's essential needs, wants and not-wants prepares you to design and deliver a presentation customized specifically for that prospect and gives you a powerful arsenal with which to strengthen your close.

And when you've additionally discovered your prospect's true readiness and ability to acquire your product, you can formulate a more efficient overall strategy and unfold your presentation and close at an appropriate rate and intensity.

Qualifying is at the very core of the sales process.
When poorly done or omitted altogether, it sets up
both you and your prospect for an irrelevant
presentation and a rough and rocky road ahead.
When properly done, it lays open the path for
effective, meaningful presentations and a high
percentage of successfully completed sales.
The road to Super Salesmanship is paved with
caring and thorough Qualifying.

Super Summary
Step Three: Qualifying

- Qualifying is discovering your prospect's needs, wants, readiness and ability to buy your product, service or idea.

- Address your questions *first* to the prospect's *needs and wants*.

  - Demonstrate an attitude of interest.

  - Listen carefully to your prospect's answers.

  - Be thinking ahead, patterning your upcoming presentation to be in alignment with your prospect's requirements as he reveals them to you.

  - Reinforce his preferences whenever his preferences are good and workable.

  - Keep asking questions until you know enough specifics about his needs, wants, not-wants and limitations to know which product will be best to present and how best to present it.

  - Ask as many questions as it takes to discover his Key Motivation for needing and/or wanting your product.

  - Take special note of this key reason for needing and/or wanting your product, to use as powerful material in your upcoming presentation and close.

more. . .

- Help the prospect, when necessary, to develop an awareness of his needs and wants.

- Discover, or help your prospect to define, his expectations, and then plan to exceed them.

- Ask blatant questions concerning the prospect's *readiness and ability* to buy only *after* you've addressed his needs and wants sufficiently to establish yourself as caring and credible.

- Consider all available data when judging your prospect's ability to buy. Do not prejudge it from appearance alone.

- Approach your prospect's readiness and ability to buy from the viewpoint, "How much more ready and able could I help him become?"

- Be prepared to modify your presentation and close according to any late-breaking data your prospect may reveal as you go along.

6

STEP FOUR: PRESENTING

N ow that you have discovered a sufficient amount of relevant data about your prospect to proceed, you are ready to present your product to your prospect.

Presenting can be defined as the process of enlightening a prospect about a product, service or idea which you intend for him to buy from you.

The goal of presenting is reached when your prospect has developed a strong enough interest in what you are offering to want to acquire it.

To help make sure that your prospect will want to buy your product from you when you've finished, here are a few key guidelines you should follow during your presentation.

The two major objectives to aim for when preparing and executing your presentation are:

Objective #1: The prospect developing a clear *understanding of* and high degree of *familiarity with* your product; and

Objective #2: The prospect developing a high level of *certainty* that your product will adequately *satisfy his particular requirements.*

NOTE: This second objective is the more senior of the two.

DEVELOPING FAMILIARITY*

To get your prospect familiar with your product,

> ### Make your product really real to your prospect.

Don't just explain and tell him about it. *Show* it to him. Make it as *hands-on* and graphic an experience as possible.

Get Him Involved

If your product is a "thing," like a bottle of mineral oil, in addition to *telling* him how it'll remove his wrinkles, brighten his outlook and send any parasites he might have scampering for the nearest exit, *show* him the bottle, point out the label and its list of super-powerful ingredients. Show him some promotional literature and testimonials supporting its miraculous claims. Hand the bottle over to him so he gets the feel of it. If it happens to taste good, you can also offer him a sample.

---

* Data contained in the section DEVELOPING FAMILIARITY and in the boxed sections in Keep Him on Track, regarding making the product real, avoiding misunderstood words, and introducing the product gradually to your prospect, are based upon educational principles contained in L. Ron Hubbard's article, BARRIERS TO STUDY. [9]

Make your presentation as hands-on as possible. Get the prospect to see, touch, hold, listen to, taste, operate, wear or step into your product.

Don't just point out and tell him about your newest model of speed-boat. Take him for the most mist-in-his-face, brine-in-his-nostrils, thrilling ride of his life. (A little "sizzle" can go a very long way toward making the sale.)

If your product is too awkward or too large to carry with you—like a herd of cattle—or too far away to take your prospect to see—like prime beach front on the coast of Barbados—carry a good representation of it, such as some pictures or a video tape.

When you don't have the thing itself at hand, use models, photos, illustrations, easy-to-understand charts, tables, diagrams or whatever you can to make your presentation as real as possible to your prospect.

If your product is not a thing but a service, the principle is still the same. Whether the service is dog-grooming or chimney sweeping or adjusting bones of the spine, you should make your presentation as real as possible.

If you don't have the dog, chimney or a model of a straightened spine to hand, show the prospect before-and-after pictures of Fido, or of a soot-filled and then soot-free chimney, or show the patient X-rays, photos or illustrations of a crooked versus a properly straightened spine.

DEVELOPING UNDERSTANDING

To make certain that your prospect gets a clear understanding of your product, be sure to

> **Make your presentation simple,
> digestible and interesting.**

Keep Him on Track

A vital point to keep in mind here is that in almost all cases, *you* know a lot more about your product than your prospect does. Therefore, you need to take special care to not confuse or lose him by trying to present your product too quickly or too steeply for him to follow you.

Keep in excellent communication with your prospect, continually observing and checking as needed whether he is still tracking with you as you go along.

EXAMPLE:

SALESMAN: (observing prospect looking fuzzy) "Did you get that last point?"

PROSPECT: "Not the last part of the money-back guarantee."

SALESMAN: "Thanks for letting me know. Let's go over the money-back guarantee again . . ."

Bear in mind your prospect's level of sophistication. Always try to

> **Avoid introducing unnecessary terms that might
> be too technical or too insider for a prospect,
> or are words that for any reason might
> be difficult for him to understand.**

and

> **If you do find that you have introduced any terms that your prospect does not fully understand, define them immediately.**

Similarly, try to

> **Introduce concepts in a smooth, gradient order, each new conceptual level building upon the earlier ones.**

Just as you wouldn't want to get lost in the fog of having "Russian 102" presented to you before you were thoroughly exposed to the basics of "Russian 101," be careful never to present advanced concepts of your products to your prospects until *after* you're satisfied they have grasped the more basic underlying ones.

Agreeable Is Easier to Digest

As always, try to remain as agreeable as you honestly can.

> **Present you, your product and your company in their best possible light.**

EXAMPLES:

- If your company is the most reputable, or best established in the industry, don't hesitate to say so.

- If you make it a regular practice to follow-up with every sale, to make sure all of your customers are completely satisfied, don't keep that a secret.

Be sure to take into consideration what you've learned about the likes and dislikes of this particular prospect.

EXAMPLES:

- If your prospect seems timid and tells you that she is a Sunday-school teacher, it wouldn't be a good idea, while demonstrating a vacuum cleaner, to roll up your sleeves and give her a bird's-eye view of what your tattoo of the naked mermaid does when you flex your biceps!

- If your prospect makes it known that he is very patriotic, don't overlook the opportunity to point out that the carpet you are trying to sell him was made in the USA, and not in Iraq, Iran or Afghanistan.

• • • • •

YOU'VE COME TO THE RIGHT PRODUCT

The second and more important of the two major objectives, when planning and executing your presentation, is to

> *Aim for the prospect to develop a high level of certainty that your product or service will, at a minimum, adequately satisfy his most important requirement(s).*

The following are the key essentials to implement in your presentation. These will ensure that your prospects do develop such a high level of certainty:

Use What You've Learned

Use what you've learned about your prospect's needs, wants and don't-wants to select which of your products or services to present.

For example, if he told you that his Key Motivation is to impress his girlfriend, Mitzi, and that she loves "fast, sleek and bright" but hates "old, loud and long," show him the brand-new red sports car, not the brown 1978 van conversion with the high-volume exhaust pipes.

Build Up the Value of Your Product

Customize your presentation to stress those features of your product which particularly benefit your prospect's most important need(s) and want(s):

SALESMAN: "This baby has the big engine" (feature)
"She does zero-to-sixty in only . . ." (benefit)

Get Your Prospect's Agreement

*"You're looking for agreement.
This is the key to SALESMANSHIP."* [10]
L. Ron Hubbard

Get your prospect's agreement at every juncture and on every major point that you make. Ask for it if necessary:

SALESMAN: "So, does this machine fly or what?"

PROSPECT: "It sure does. This machine is fast. Mitzi'll love it."

NOTE: This principle of getting your prospects' agreement is so basic and powerful, it looms high above most others in its ability to get a product sold.

Sell the Sizzle

If there are things which are very special or potentially exciting and desirable about your product, service or company, which you have no reason to believe would be offensive to your prospect, be sure to include them in your presentation:

SALESMAN: "This beauty comes equipped with a state-of-the-art, digital, six-speaker sound system that'll knock her socks off. Here, give *this* a listen."

While much of the rest of your presentation might appeal to the prospect's sense of logic, *selling the sizzle* can add dramatic impact which can go directly to your prospect's heart and soul. That *emotional* involvement can be the deciding factor of the sale:

PROSPECT: "That was totally awesome. I definitely want this one."

Be Sure the Full Audience Is in the Theater

Before starting your presentation, do whatever you appropriately can to be certain you have ALL "decision makers" in attendance. By "decision maker" is meant anyone and everyone whose input would be needed for a buying decision to be made. Prime suspect among them would be the person's spouse (if they have one).

If you proceed into your presentation knowingly or unknowingly without all decision makers present, you open the door to a world of complication. You have the real likelihood that you will be unable to close the sale at the conclusion of your presentation and that you may have to redo the presentation—if you get the chance—to subsequently include the missing decision maker(s), before a sale can be made. And, before you can redo the presentation, your prospect is very apt to relay to the other decision maker(s), in a haphazard fashion, what you had presented to him in a carefully orchestrated manner.

Additionally, you can lose all of the emotional impact of any sizzle you've introduced into the original presentation. You are also likely to lose any timely advantage you might have gained through the use of any closing ammunition involving urgency (like: "If you buy *now*, I'll throw in an extended warranty").

If the sale of your product or service is the sort that often requires more than one decision maker, it is worth the extra effort to try to have all decision makers present before starting your presentation.

EXAMPLE:

SALESMAN: "Mr. Rosser, before I begin presenting this pipe organ to you, is there anyone else we should be including in here, like perhaps Mrs. Rosser, *or anyone else that you might need to consult with before making a buying decision?*"

PROSPECT: "No. I'm good to go on my own."

SALESMAN: (confirming) "Okay then. So, if you like what you see and hear and decide to go ahead, *there's no one else that you'd need to consult with to make a decision?*"

PROSPECT: "That's right. Now, lemme hear some Bach comin' through those pipes and maybe I'll take one of these babies home with me."

SALESMAN: "You've got it."

EXAMPLE:

SALESMAN: "*. . . is there anyone else you might need to consult with before making a buying decision?*"

PROSPECT: "Well, I'm of course not sure yet whether I'd want to buy it or not, but if I do decide I like it, I would then need to have my wife, Andrea, as well as my daughter, Susie, who is the family musician, in on the decision."

SALESMAN: "No problem whatsoever. How about we call them and invite them to pop right over here and join us for the presentation. You and I can have a cup of coffee while we wait."

Your best chance of closing a sale is right at the conclusion of your presentation. It is almost axiomatic that: *The more time that elapses between your presentation and your buyer's commitment, the less chance there is that there will be a commitment.* So . . . try to have all decision makers present before beginning your grand performance.

Stay on the Mark

Don't dwell on the explanations of features which are not needed or wanted by, or points which are not especially of interest to, the particular prospect in front of you. Keep your presentation as pertinent as possible. Your presentation will be as penetrating as it is pertinent.

You will keep the prospect's interest to the degree that you continue to show him features of your product or service that *offer the exact benefits* which *he* is seeking. You will be successful in your presentation to the degree that you convincingly demonstrate to him how these features will *satisfy the exact needs and wants* he has for the product or service.

Save the Worst for Last

If the best product you have to offer has some features known to be undesirable to your prospect, don't point out those features until *after* you've properly pointed out how well the product *does* fulfill his requirements.

Consider the Prospect's Parameters

Whenever possible, try to select a product which fits within the prospect's limitations. When only a product beyond his means will serve, go ahead and present the product, knowing that before the sale is over, you may have to help him stretch his limits to enable him to buy your product.

Show Your Conviction

> *"Making somebody want something they really need is no crime . . ."*[11]
> L. Ron Hubbard

Let your prospect know how much you sincerely believe in your product and your company and how right you truly believe they are for him. Share the depth and detail of your enthusiasm. The more he observes your conviction in your wares and in your organization, the more confidence he will tend to develop and the more secure he will be with his decision to buy your product.

Fortify the credibility of your product as needed with testimonials or other documentation.

Continue to Present

Your presentation is complete when your prospect has developed a strong enough interest in your product, service or idea to want to acquire it. Until you get your prospect to that point, your job is to continue to present it to him and handle any sales resistance that may come up along the way.

If you can manage to do this, regardless of any and all obstacles, you are going to be an extremely successful salesperson.

In the upcoming chapters, I'll be showing you *exactly how to handle anything* that might come up and how to do it with finesse.

• • • • •

When you take the care to present your products in ways that ensure your prospects gain a clear understanding of and thorough familiarity with them, and a strong conviction that your products will fulfill their specific needs and wants, you're going to discover yourself with a lot of prospects who have developed a strong interest in and desire to own your products.

The road to Super Salesmanship is paved with clear, penetrating presentations. When done with skill and care, your presentations can be filled with fun and lead to many successfully completed sales.

SUPER SUMMARY
Step Four: Presenting

- Use what you've learned about your prospect's requirements to select which of your products or services to present.

- Give your prospect a clear *understanding* of and a high level of *familiarity* with your product.
  - Keep it simple, digestible and interesting.
    - Move forward at a pace that's comfortable for him.
    - Avoid unnecessary use of words that are likely to be difficult for him to understand, and immediately define any words that he does not fully understand.
  - Get the prospect involved with the product.
    - Use the product itself, or as real a representation as you can have on hand, to demonstrate.
    - Have him experience it as hands-on as possible.

- Convincingly demonstrate to your prospect how your product will adequately satisfy his most important requirements.
  - Have all decision makers in attendance for the presentation.

more. . .

- Present your product, yourself and your company in their best light, taking into consideration what you've learned about the prospect's likes and dislikes.

- Establish the product's value and credibility.

- Stress those features which specifically benefit this particular prospect.

- Sell the Sizzle—Present any special or dramatic features of your product and company which you believe will impress and possibly excite your prospect.

- Express the depth of your conviction that your product and organization are right for him.

- Gain as much agreement from the prospect as you can.

- Continue to present until your prospect has developed a strong interest in, and desire to acquire, your product or service.

"Don't try to overwhelm. Penetrate."[12]

—L. Ron Hubbard

7

STEP FIVE: CLOSING

O nce the prospect has developed a strong interest to own your product, it's time for you to close the sale.

Closing is defined as getting a firm commitment from the prospect to acquire the product or service which is being offered.

This would include all applicable paperwork completed and signed, as well as payment made or financial arrangements fully in place.

You are going to find closing as smooth and satisfying an experience as:

1) You've gotten all four of the earlier steps of the sale thoroughly laid in place; and

2) You are willing and able to skillfully and caringly handle any and all *objections** that surface along the way.

---

* Objections—An objection is a reason or concern the prospect has his attention on which is causing him to hesitate committing to the sale.

First we'll look at a couple of techniques to smoothly secure a firm commitment when the prospect is not particularly resisting the process. Then we'll look at what works when he is being resistive.

CLOSING SIGNAL

Many if not most times, the prospect will give you a sign toward the conclusion of the presentation, if not sooner (commonly called a "closing signal"), that he has made a decision and is ready to buy your product or service.

EXAMPLES:

- "Do you accept personal checks?"
- "Yep, I'm convinced."
- "Where do I sign up?"
- "How soon could you deliver 10,000 of those widgets?"

Such a signal can come ANYWHERE along the way, and a salesperson should always be alert for it.

A VITAL rule is that

> ***When you receive a closing signal, no matter where it comes in the sales process, you cease all other activity and go directly into the close.***

EXAMPLE:

SALESMAN: "Which color would you prefer?"

PROSPECT: "Oh, that red one is gorgeous. *I'm sold. Let's do it.*"

SALESMAN: "*You bet. Follow me. I'll introduce you to our friendly cashier.*"

Once you've received a closing signal, if you continue moving on in any direction other than directly into the close, you risk introducing something which could give your prospect second thoughts and get in the way of the sale.

EXAMPLE:

PROSPECT: "That red one is gorgeous. *I'm sold. Let's do it.*"

SALESMAN: "Yes, red *and blue* are our most popular colors. But *we're out of stock on the blue right now.*"

PROSPECT: "Oh, *it also comes in blue? Why don't we hold off* until you get the blue back in stock. I might as well take a look at it."

A Misread Sign

Sometimes what seemed to be a closing signal will turn out not to have been one.

There will be occasions when you get what you perceive to be a closing signal and move directly into the close, only to then discover you misread the signal:

SALESMAN: "Isn't this one in dusty blue irresistible?"

PROSPECT: "Okay. *Say no more. You've convinced me.*"

SALESMAN: "Good. Are you planning to pay by cash or check?"

PROSPECT: "Pay? I'm not ready to *pay!* You've simply convinced me that blue is definitely the right color for me! Now, can you show me some more models in that shade of blue?"

At such times, you simply backtrack to where you were before receiving what you thought was the closing signal and continue forward from there:

SALESMAN: "No problem. Step right over here and I'll be glad to show you the other models that come in dusty blue."

There are other times when you *do* read the signal correctly and move into the close, but because the closing signal caused you to cut short or altogether skip earlier steps, the close doesn't go smoothly:

SALESMAN: (While Presenting) "This model has a lot of features which would fit well with your needs and comes in green, as you see it, as well as in blue."

PROSPECT: "That green one is exactly, precisely and unquestionably the one I want. I've been shopping for a long time and don't need to go over the features or have it demonstrated to me. *Let's just sit down and do it.*"

SALESMAN: "You got it. Would you prefer to pay by check, credit card or financing?"

PROSPECT: "Well, what's the total cost?"

SALESMAN: "$17,311."

PROSPECT: *"Whoa! Whoa!! Whoa!!!* I had no idea the price was so high. That seems like a lot of money for that model."

To get the sale back into motion, you simply backtrack to the step you were on when you received the closing signal and bring the action forward again from there:

SALESMAN: (Going back to Presenting) "I understand how it might *seem* like a lot of money. But, if you'll bear with me, I'd like to take a couple of moments to go over some very special features on this particular model so you can see how much benefit and value they actually do offer you."

So, even though you may have to backtrack after mistaking something else for a closing signal, and even though you may sometimes, after receiving a legitimate closing signal, run into trouble for skipping steps when moving into the close, you will nonetheless find it is a VERY successful policy to *move directly into the close whenever you receive a closing signal.*

Most of the time you will be right and you will close your sale.

NO CLOSING SIGNAL

For those times when you reach the end of your presentation and you have not yet received any closing signal, there are a couple of highly workable techniques which can smoothly bridge you and your prospect over from the presentation into the close.

Trial Close

Directly asking for the sale: "Are you ready to buy?" without *knowing* how ready your prospect is to commit, can unnecessarily invite him to give you a "No" response.

A trial close is a way to "ask for the sale" without actually *asking* for the sale. It's a question you ask, the answer to which lets you know how ready the prospect is or isn't to make a firm commitment:

SALESMAN: "So, *what do you think of this model?*"

PROSPECT: "I like it. I like it a lot. If you have it in red, I'll take it."

If your prospect responds with a closing signal, as this one did, you follow the cardinal rule: Cease all other activity and go directly into the close.

> SALESMAN: "We sure do have it in red. *Would you prefer to pay by credit card or check?*"

If, on the other hand, you receive a response that is NOT a closing signal (e.g., "I like it, but it's not quite right for me."), simply apply the following four-step formula:

1) **CLARIFY** the nature of the response, as needed;

2) **ACKNOWLEDGE** the response with understanding;

3) **HANDLE** appropriately; and then

4) **TRY AGAIN** to close the sale.

EXAMPLE:

> SALESMAN: "So, what do you think of this model?"
>
> PROSPECT: "It's not quite right for me."
>
> SALESMAN: "I see. Well, may I ask you what it is about this model that seems not quite right for you?" (Clarify)
>
> PROSPECT: "I like it, but it's a little too noisy for me."
>
> SALESMAN: "Thank you for letting me know of that concern." (Acknowledgement) "We have that same model here in the 'whisper-soft' version and at the same price." (Handle) *"How does that seem to you?"* (Trial Close)
>
> PROSPECT: "Sounds great. If you have it in burgundy, I'll take it." (Closing Signal)
>
> SALESMAN: "We do have it in burgundy. Follow me and I'll introduce you to the cashier." (Close)

Assumptive Close

Another excellent technique which can smoothly bridge your prospect over from the conclusion of your presentation into the close is called the "assumptive close."

Here you simply *assume* that your prospect is willing to commit and you proceed into the close accordingly. You proceed forward by offering him *two positive choices:*

SALESMAN: ". . . and in summary, that's how the Model X17 will clean your carpets, peel your potatoes and help you meet and marry the mate of your dreams."

PROSPECT: "It seems like a very nice product."

SALESMAN: "It sure is. *Were you planning to finance or to purchase it outright?*"

In the next moment, the salesman will learn if he has assumed correctly:

PROSPECT: "Well, I was planning to put $3,000 down and finance the balance. Can you arrange that for me?"

In this example, the salesman *did* assume correctly, as you will find is very often the case.

OBJECTIONS

Many times, however, you will discover that your prospect is *not* ready to close. He still has unaddressed concerns or objections in mind, which are causing him to resist going forward with the purchase.

Objections can be slight or substantial, frail or formidable and can come at you at any time and in every form imaginable.

The variations of "closing techniques" which sales professionals have devised over the eons to try to overcome this seemingly infinite variety of objections are almost too numerous to list. Whole books have been written on the subject.

NOTE: One of the biggest mistakes a salesman can make in the field of selling is the mishandling of an objection that has been offered to him by his prospect. Instead of dealing with it in a fashion that would simply reduce or eliminate it out of the way of his sale, he *reacts* to it, slapping it back against the prospect, trying to overwhelm the objection by attacking it—and the prospect along with it:

> PROSPECT: "Yes, I really do want to buy it . . . but I get very uncomfortable when it gets right down to making a decision."

> SALESMAN: "What's the big deal? The whole cost is less than $500! There's nothing to decide. Just pick up the pen and sign the contract."

Such antagonistic response to an objection is not only abrasive to the prospect, it is a highly risky thing for the salesman to do. It tends to unravel the very fabric of which the salesman-prospect relationship is woven and thereby tends to undermine the sale itself.

In trying to close the sale, a salesperson should never need to resort to techniques that resist and argue with the objection.

If, in your Opening and Qualifying, you have truly penetrated through and discovered your prospect's key needs and wants; *and* in your Presentation, you've created a very real connection between those key needs and your product's ability to satisfy those needs, you will have put yourself in an excellent position to dissolve away any "Sales Resistance" that might crop up at the close, in a manner that is friendly and supportive.

The process that makes this so possible is the simple and highly workable, four-step formula:

1) CLARIFY as needed

2) ACKNOWLEDGE

3) HANDLE

4) TRY AGAIN to close the sale

This extremely effective formula will enable you to handle and dissolve away any and all objections that a legitimate prospect might voice.

We'll be taking a much closer look at applying this formula in the upcoming chapter on Handling Objections.

Two Kinds of Objections

Objections fall into two basic categories:

1) **Those that *can be handled with communication alone;* and**

2) **Those that *require an actual, "real-world" handling* before the sale can close.**

Here's an example of an objection which can be handled with communication alone:

PROSPECT: "Yes, I really do want to buy it . . . but I get very uncomfortable when it gets right down to making a decision."

SALESMAN: "I can understand that." (Acknowledgement)

"But please let me take another moment to again *reassure you* that this model has features which will fulfill . . . (all the specific needs prospect mentioned earlier) . . . and is at an unusually good price." (Handle)

> "Wouldn't it be much more convenient for you to simply get it now?" (Trial Close)

PROSPECT: "Oh . . . I know you are absolutely right. I do need it and I really do want it. Okay! I'm going to just go ahead and take it."

SALESMAN: "Very good decision. Would you prefer to pay by credit card or check?" (Close)

An example of an objection that needs some real-world handling would be:

PROSPECT: "I love the boat and I'll let you know tomorrow."

SALESMAN: "No problem. But is there some reason tomorrow would be better for you than today?" (Clarify)

PROSPECT: "Well, it's occurred to me, I don't know if my garage door is wide enough for this model to fit through. So, I'll need to go home and measure."

SALESMAN: "Very good point." (Acknowledgement)

"Is there anyone you could call at home who could measure the doorway to let us know NOW?" (Handle)

. . . a short time later . . .

PROSPECT: "My wife measured it and says it's definitely wide enough. I'll take it."

Handle With Communication

Almost always, the wisest procedure is to

> ## *Try to handle any objection with communication alone*

and to only resort to real-world solutions when communication alone will not get the job done.

Incomplete Earlier Step

It's interesting to note that an objection very often indicates that you and your prospect have an incomplete earlier step in the sales process. In such cases, you may need to backtrack and complete that earlier step before coming forward once again to try to close the sale.

EXAMPLES:

1) Need to Get Prospect More Willing to Communicate (incomplete Opening step)

Perhaps something was done or said somewhere along the way which caused your prospect to lose his willingness to communicate openly to you (if he ever really had been fully willing). It is very common for the prospect to be withholding worries, concerns and other objections from you because he has not yet reached, or is no longer at, a point where he feels *completely* safe to confide in you:

SALESMAN: "So, how did you like that model?"

PROSPECT: "I like it a lot. *Let me think about it* and I'll get back to you."

SALESMAN: "I understand. But before you leave, would you mind telling me if there is some particular reason you feel it would benefit you more to think about it than to just take the system home with you so you can start enjoying it today?" (Clarify)

PROSPECT: "Well, um, uh, well . . . to tell you the truth, I saw the same model in today's paper for $50 less at Electronics Empire." (shows ad)

Once you've gotten him willing to communicate openly, you can *acknowledge* his concern, *handle* it appropriately, and *move again toward the close:*

SALESMAN: "Thank you very much for letting me know about that." (Acknowledgement)

"Let's see here . . . In the fine print of this ad it mentions that if you want the remote control with it, there's an additional $75 charge. Since our price already includes the remote control, ours will actually cost you $25 LESS!" (Handle)

PROSPECT: "My gosh! You're right. I think I will go ahead and buy it here."

2) Need More Qualifying

Or perhaps your prospect was insufficiently qualified. When you move into your presentation *before* you've discovered enough needed-and-wanted data about your prospect, you may find you have to similarly backpedal your way out of trouble:

PROSPECT: "Well, I didn't care for ANY of the colors you've shown me."

SALESMAN: "Thank you for bringing that to my attention." (Acknowledgement)

"What colors are you most interested in?"

PROSPECT: "Purple is my number one choice and green is my second."

SALESMAN: "Boy, are we in luck. My inventory readout shows there is still one purple one left. Let's go take a look." (Handle)

PROSPECT: "Only one left, huh? I'd better grab it while I can. How do we make it mine?"

This last example, incidentally, is a good demonstration of the use of the powerful closing tool, URGENCY, in which you

> *Give your prospect an irresistible reason to close now!*

3) Need to Demonstrate More Value (incomplete Presenting step)

Or, maybe your presentation of the product didn't demonstrate enough value for him to want to buy it:

PROSPECT: "Well, the Flex-All seems like it would be great for my upper-torso and leg muscle groups, but as I mentioned earlier, I need something that can also flatten my stomach and ripple my abs."

SALESMAN: "You sure DID mention that earlier." (Acknowledgement)

"I simply forgot to show you this model's best feature. *Special attachment #8, which is included at no extra cost,* is specifically designed to flatten the tummy and ripple the abs. Here, let me show you . . ." (Handle)

PROSPECT: "That's exactly what I've been looking for. Wrap it up. I'll take it."

Everything's Been Fine . . . Up Until Now

Perhaps the objection is NOT a result of an incomplete earlier step, but is truly a response to *something that comes up at the close itself*, such as the price:

PROSPECT: "Great presentation. I'd like to buy this model if I can afford it."

SALESMAN: "Good choice. This model is only $549."

PROSPECT: "Whoops! That's what I was afraid of. It definitely seems worth it, but I think that's about three times what my budget can handle."

The handling steps for such an objection are basically the same. Once the prospect has clearly given you his objection, you acknowledge, handle and once again move to close:

SALESMAN: "I understand." (Acknowledgement)

"But I really want you to have it. Would it help if the company agreed to divide the cost into three equal monthly payments?" (Proposed Handle as a Trial Close)

PROSPECT: "Oh, that would be wonderful. If you could arrange that, I'd take it."

But What if I'm Wrong?

Or maybe the objection is a common case of "fear-of-making-the-wrong-decision" setting in emotionally on the prospect, as it all too often does when it gets threateningly close to decision time. Keep a "watchful ear" out for this, because most often when this fear objection surfaces, the prospect will try to obscure it with a *smoke screen* of invented excuses:

PROSPECT: "Okay, so before I can say yes, I'll need to double-check my schedule, make sure my wife's fine with this, triple-check my budget situation, confirm that my astrological indicators are all in alignment and then . . . I'll need to think about it some more."

SALESMAN: "I can understand your hesitance to make this commitment. And I really do want you to be comfortable with your decision. But I just want to clarify something. Is there any other reason you're hesitating?"

PROSPECT: "Well, um . . . I really do need and want it . . . but, um, truthfully *I just think I may be making a wrong decision.*"

Being able to recognize the exact emotional state, or tone, a person is in, such as being in fear, and knowing exactly what to do about it, are very valuable skills to have in selling, as well as in life itself.*

If you discover that fear-of-making-the-wrong-decision is stopping your prospect from taking the steps necessary to secure the product he needs, it is your job as his Super Salesperson to

> ### *Give him all the reassurance he needs to get him past his fear*

so he can acquire the product and solve his problem:

---

* The best tools I have ever come across for helping one spot and understand a person's emotional tone level are: The Tone Scale, which gives the entire range of emotions (such as fear, anxiety, anger, boredom) as presented in L. Ron Hubbard's article, TONE SCALE IN FULL,[13] and The Chart of Human Evaluation, as presented in L. Ron Hubbard's book, *Science of Survival*.[14]

SALESMAN: "I completely understand and I appreciate you letting me know that." (Acknowledgement)

"I want to again reassure you that this model will easily fulfill . . . (each of the important needs he's confided in you) . . . and it fits well within your budget. I want you to know how strongly I feel that this is the right thing for you. If you were my own father, I'd tell you that the best thing you could do would be to go ahead with this." (Handle with Reassurance)

PROSPECT: "I know you're right. And I know I really do need it . . . Okay! I'm going to go ahead and take it."

SALESMAN: (while extending his arm for a handshake) "You've made a very good decision. Have a seat and we'll work out the details." (Close)

Bring in the Cavalry—Testimonials and Other Second Opinions

Sometimes your personal assurance is not enough to convince the prospect to move ahead. In such cases, another extremely effective closing technique is to

> ***Bring in additional opinions which fortify the viewpoint and give your prospect the reassurance that a decision to buy is the right thing to do.***

We all seem to feel much more comfortable making a buying decision when we know that other people agree with the wisdom of our decision. And the more wholeheartedly they agree with us, the better we seem to feel about it.

Testimonials

One way to apply this principle is to

> ### *Show your prospect written testimonials from other customers*

who did go ahead and purchase the product and who are now extremely glad that they did.

Because these testimonials can be so valuable to you, you should make it a regular practice to ask for them whenever you have a customer who seems sincerely pleased with the outcome of his purchase. The very best time to ask for and get such a pleased customer to write a testimonial for you is at the precise time that they are expressing their pleasure and delight.

CUSTOMER: "Deede, I again want to thank you for taking such good care of us and seeing to it that we got the one that will keep us happy for years."

SALESMAN: "It's been my pleasure, Mr. Callahan. I have a favor to ask. Would you be kind enough to take a minute or two right now and write up how you feel about doing business with me and my company and about your new houseboat?"

You can keep the presentation of these testimonials simple by collecting them up and keeping them in a handy file for such times as when they are needed. Or you might do it with a bit more style by having your customers write their testimonials on fine paper and keeping them in plastic sleeves in a good quality binder.

And, as mentioned in the last chapter, you don't have to wait until the close to share these reassuring testimonials with your prospects. You can bring them to your prospects' attention at will or just keep the binder at arm's-reach in a strategic location, such as a reception area, to be picked up and browsed through by prospects at any time during the sales procedure.

Second Opinions

Another, even more powerful version of this technique, for use when needed as a closing tool, is to

> ### *Get some particularly enthusiastic customers to give their testimonials in person.*

This can be done by getting them to agree to remain on stand-by, to be called upon by you and your prospects (or directly by your prospects, in cases when it seems more effective for you not to be present) to share their glowing testimonials and give their comforting reassurances—in person or over the phone. This version of the Testimonials technique is sometimes known as a "Vouch" or "Tag."

It is ideal to prearrange to have several such satisfied customer "Vouchers" available who will attest to the wonderfulness of you, your company and your product. It's a good idea to have a variety of types at hand so that you can match prospect types to satisfied customer types. E.g.: A conservative senior citizen might respect the opinion of a fellow senior citizen more than that of a teenager with spiked-up purple hair and a ring through his nose . . . and vice versa!

You can use others, besides your customers, for Vouches as well. For example, you can call on *co-workers* and *outside experts* for a second opinion:

PROSPECT: "I appreciate your opinion, but I still don't know if these shoes really go well with this dress."

SALESMAN: "Well, Mona right over there is our Senior Style Consultant. Let's ask her.

"Oh, Mona, could you please come over here for a moment and tell us what you think of these shoes with this dress? I think they're a good match, but Daisy's not sure."

MONA: "Totally exquisite. They're a perfect compliment for one another."

PROSPECT: "You really think so?"

MONA: "Honey, those shoes were made for that dress. You better grab them up, quick."

PROSPECT: "I'll take them."

Because effective objection handling is such a vital part of Super Salesmanship, I have included an entire chapter, "Handling Objections and Other Troubleshooting," in which we will take another much closer look at the simple, yet penetrating, step-by-step method for handling any and all objections that may ever come your way.

SOME REQUIRE CULTIVATION

While many sales can potentially be completed during the initial meeting, sometimes a sale, by happenstance or by design, takes more than one go-round to close.

Many big-ticket items, such as a large real-estate transaction or the sale of a fleet of jet planes, for example, will ordinarily take a number of meetings and an extended period of time before the sale is finally completed.

Your best guarantee for keeping an in-progress sale moving smoothly forward is to

> ***Keep in excellent communication
> with all involved parties.***

This not only keeps the relationship strong and healthy, it also allows you to continually coordinate progress toward completing the sale. Additionally, keeping in good communication enables you to detect any problems that might be developing, thus giving you the opportunity to address and resolve them before they can grow large enough to sabotage the sale.

THE BUCK STOPS HERE

There are many fields, such as new car sales, real estate sales and a variety of professional practices, in which the individual who has been fulfilling the function of "salesperson" turns over part or all of the final closing functions to someone else.

Once the salesperson has secured a firm commitment from his prospective customer, client, or patient, in many fields it is customary to turn the prospect over to another department or individual, such as a Cashier or Finance Manager, for the actual arranging of the financing, collection of the money, and/or filling out of the sale's documentation.

It should be noted that regardless of how many individuals or departments are involved in the transaction, until the monies are collected in full (or firm financial arrangements are locked into place, assuring payment in full) and all required documentation has been properly completed and signed, the sale is not fully "closed" and the salesperson's job is not yet fully "done."

THREE KEYS TO SUCCESSFUL CLOSES

Your close will be as smooth and successful as you are thorough with the following keys:

1) Create a relationship with your prospect in which your prospect has built up enough trust in you to allow you to discover his most needed and wanted reason(s) for acquiring your product or service.

2) Deliver a highly relevant presentation in which you honestly and convincingly demonstrate how the features of your product will fulfill the specific needs and wants your prospect has for your product.

3) Always remain aware that the goal of your efforts and your mission as a salesperson is to get a firm, signed, sealed and financially secured commitment from your prospect to acquire the product. And *persist* in your efforts, including the reducing away of any and all resistance that comes up, until you get that firm commitment or until your prospect is truly no longer a legitimate prospect for your product.

The path to Super Salesmanship is caringly paved with an ascending set of skillfully laid steps, upon which successful closes are built.

SUPER SUMMARY
Step Five: Closing

- Closing is defined as getting a firm commitment, including completed paperwork and payment, from the prospect to acquire the product or service you are offering.

- *Whenever* you receive a "closing signal," go directly into the close.

- If at the conclusion of your presentation, the prospect gives no closing signal:

  - Use the "assumptive close": Assume that the prospect is willing to commit and proceed directly into a close by offering him two positive choices.

  - To confirm a prospect's level of readiness to commit, use a "trial close."

- Use urgency to encourage the prospect to commit immediately.

- Handle any and all objections which surface with this four-step system:
  1) Recognize or get clarified the nature of the objection.

2) Acknowledge it with understanding.

3) Handle it appropriately.

Backtrack and complete any incomplete, earlier steps as needed.

4) Proceed forward and close the sale.

- Try to handle all objections with communication alone. Only resort to real-world solutions when communication alone fails to get the job done.

- Bring in the opinions of others, if needed, to fortify your personal assurances that buying is the winning thing to do.

- *Persist, persist, persist* until you close your sale or until your prospect is truly no longer a legitimate prospect for your product or service.

8
FOLLOW-THROUGH

Your customer has said "Yes!" He wants to buy your product. He's given you his firm commitment. You've gotten your contract signed and payment secured. You've *closed* your sale.

Very well done!

But don't relax your "sales muscles" just yet. Your job as a Super Salesman is not quite complete.

Now is the time to *follow through* on your sale. In addition to benefiting your customer, proper follow-through will increase opportunities for future business and minimize the possibility of back-out attempts.

The following are key, time-tested tips that will help maximize the effectiveness of your follow-through:

GIVE REASSURANCE

Customers can have second thoughts, known as "Buyer's Remorse," in which their certainty that they have made the right decision wanes and they consider reneging or refunding.

As we saw in the previous chapter on Closing, a decision is sometimes a frail thing:

"Uh, well, maybe, yeah, okay. I guess I'll go ahead and take it."

People like to be right and are often afraid of being wrong. When your customer has made a commitment to buy, you should

> ***Immediately start giving him solid reassurance that he has made the right decision.***

A hearty "Congratulations" and a firm handshake, while getting the contract signed and payment secured, are a good beginning. And continuing to reassure your prospect as necessary throughout your follow-up contacts is also a good practice.

DELIVER THE GOODS

Your Customer Expected "Good" and Got "Great"

When a customer's expectations are *exceeded*, he tends to:

- Bring his business back for more;
- Give your company a good name; and
- Send referrals to the salesman.

As you prepare to deliver your product or service, take a moment to evaluate how your customer is likely to be viewing the service you have thus far provided to him.

Today's customers do not expect superb service from their salespeople. They are generally grateful to simply get through the experience without too much wear and tear on their patience and their pocketbooks. The average, and even the somewhat above-average, salesperson tends to have neither the interest nor the real willingness to go the extra mile in order to exceed his or her customer's expectations.

You, on the other hand, will find that if you simply have done a first-rate job of directing your customer through the five steps of Super Salesmanship, as laid out in these chapters, you have already surpassed the expectations of 95% of today's customers.

If you have: shown the sincere interest and good communication skills it takes to get a customer into trusting, open communication; done a thorough job of discovering your customer's most vital needs and wants; custom designed and delivered a convincing presentation of how you, your organization and your product will more than adequately satisfy his needs and wants; and have successfully assisted your customer to overcome any and all barriers which threatened to keep him from acquiring your product or service . . . you have certainly surpassed the expectations of most any customer you might serve.

Now, as you prepare to get the product or service delivered, you have another excellent opportunity to place a fine finishing touch onto your sales performance.

Deliver in Abundance

". . . try to give better than expected quality. Deliver and get paid for it, for sure, but deliver better than was ordered and more. Always try to write a better story than was expected; always try to deliver a better job than was ordered. Always try to—and deliver—a better result than what was hoped for." [16]

L. Ron Hubbard

Do it Early, More, Better, Special

Just as you have gone the extra mile and done more than simply an "adequate" job of caring for your customer as you moved him through the steps of the sale, here again, when you deliver your product or service to him, try to do something special to exceed what your customer is expecting.

If he is anxious to receive it, do everything you can to make sure it gets delivered even *earlier* than promised.

If there is some legitimate way to deliver *more* quantity than agreed upon, do it. If you sold him a dozen bagels, make it thirteen. If the print job called for 5,000 pieces, deliver 5,500.

Another way to exceed expectations is to deliver *higher quality* than sold and expected. If you sold an RV (recreational vehicle) to include a basic DVD setup, surprise and delight him by including a full five-speaker sound system.

Don't spare the creativity. When you prepare to deliver, *make it special*. If they bought a new car for their mom for her birthday, have it covered with ribbons and balloons and a big "Happy Birthday" banner when they bring her by to pick it up. If they bought an oil change, throw in a free car wash. Upon closing a nice deal, give your customer a pair of theater tickets or a gift certificate for dinner at a fine restaurant. If it's a "big-deal," like the sale of a major piece of real estate, cap it off with a new TV or a Hawaiian vacation for two.

An extra special gesture or two at delivery can go a long way toward making up for any earlier shortcomings, and can turn your delivery into a memorable one that leaves a lasting, positive impression.

Customer Satisfaction Index

At the end of each major phase of your sales relationship with your customer, and especially at the conclusion of the delivery, it is an important practice to

> ***Be very sure you haven't left your prospect with any expectations that have not been addressed or met.***

EXAMPLE:

SALESMAN: "Did we get everything taken care of to your satisfaction?"

CUSTOMER: "Pretty much. Though, you mentioned you knew of a good tax attorney you would put me in touch with."

SALESMAN: "That I did. Thanks for reminding me. Here's his card with full contact information. And feel free to mention my name. If you wish, I'll call him ahead and tell him to expect your call."

CUSTOMER: "I would really appreciate that."

SALESMAN: (while writing self a note to make the call) "Consider it done. Anything else you were hoping for that we haven't gotten to or we've left incomplete?"

CUSTOMER: "No, Max. You've done everything you said you would and more and I appreciate it very much. You'll see more of my business, when the time comes, and I'll be sending you some referrals as well."

SALESMAN: (shaking hands, followed by handing customer a bunch of business cards) "It's been
my pleasure, Gary. And let me give you a few
of my business cards for you to hand out to
those you refer."

The practice of checking for expectations and making sure
they are, at a minimum, met, is one of the qualities that sepa-
rates the average salesman from the outstanding salesman. And
deciding to go the extra mile to *exceed* the prospect's expectations can elevate the outstanding salesman into the ranks of the
extraordinary.

Do It As Soon As Possible

Whether or not your prospect has included rapid delivery as
an expectation, a vital policy, in general, is to

> ***Deliver the product or provide the***
> ***service you've sold as quickly as***
> ***is practically possible.***

You want your customer to take possession and begin to actually
experience and benefit from the product as rapidly as possible.
That way everyone wins.

There is also a potential liability in allowing a delayed delivery. In the absence of the product to experience, your customer
has an elevated temptation to question the wisdom of his decision. He has made a commitment and perhaps already handed
over some real money, but has not yet received anything real in
exchange. This is all the more so if others in his environment
question the wisdom of his decision. You could end up hearing
your customer saying things like these:

CUSTOMER: "I'm not sure if I should get that acupuncture program I signed up for after all. The waitress at the corner diner says that the head dishwasher told her he thinks it's a form of VooDoo."

CUSTOMER: ". . . and then my neighbor said, 'You bought a WHAT? A set of bright pink and purple lawn furniture? Are you out of your mind?'"

Whether rapid delivery has taken place or not, be sure to keep in excellent communication with your customer. That way you can detect and nip in the bud any remorseful thoughts he may be having, reconfirm the wisdom of his decision and keep enthusiasm alive.

FOLLOW-UP CALL

Making a follow-up call, usually two to five days after closing the sale and delivering the product or service, is a very wise thing to do.

It lets your customer know that you are still there for him, that you didn't disappear the moment he signed on the dotted line.

Congratulate him again and ask him how he is enjoying the product. Pick up any questions, concerns or confusions he may be sitting with regarding his purchase.

> *Anything that comes up during the follow-up should be handled fully and as quickly as possible:*

SALESMAN: "I can understand your concern over your neighbor's comments. But didn't you select pink and purple because they are YOUR favorite colors? And by the way, isn't that the same neighbor who claims Mother Theresa wore her robes too short?"

CUSTOMER: "Yes, you're right. My neighbor, Rita, does take the term *conservatism* to a whole new extreme. And, yes, pink and purple are my favorite colors and everyone besides 'Reactionary Rita' just LOVES the set lounging around my pool. I guess I really am happy with it."

GET REFERRALS

As we noted in Chapter 3, Prospecting, a satisfied customer can be one of your richest (and least costly) sources of additional business. Not only is he himself a prime candidate for future repeat sales, but in the meanwhile he might have some quality referrals he can send your way.

There is probably no time when your customer will be more enthusiastic about you and your product than when he's just taken delivery of the product or received the service.

Asking him, "Who else do you know that might benefit similarly?" can get you some excellent referrals.

Once you've fully handled any concerns there may have been and confirmed that your customer is pleased with you and your product, you might wish to take that very ripe moment to ask for additional referrals:

SALESMAN: "How are you enjoying your new purchase?"

CUSTOMER: "I couldn't be more pleased."

SALESMAN: "I always enjoy hearing that, Peggy. *Who else do you know that you'd like to see benefit similarly?*"

Note down the particulars. Get correctly spelled names, addresses, phone numbers, e-mail addresses, etc., so you will be able to take proper action.

Before concluding your follow-up call, reassure your customer that you intend to remain stably in the relationship:

". . . Please call me with any questions or concerns. I'm at your service."

KEEP IN TOUCH

It's an excellent practice to maintain a "tickler file" to systematically remind yourself to

> ***Follow up at regular intervals and
> for special occasions***

(e.g., one, six and twelve months after the sale, holidays, customer's birthday, etc.) with a call or note.

You can use some of these as opportunities to ask for additional referrals in one creative way or another. Perhaps offer a gift certificate or "bird dog" (referral fee) as an incentive, or maybe a discount on future purchases as a reward. A periodic letter or newsletter to all customers can be effective for keeping them informed and feeling valued.

Staying in such good communication will also increase your customers' loyalty, so when they find themselves back in the market, they will most likely call on *you*.

*The road to Super Salesmanship is an upwardly
spiraling journey in which swift, cheerful, first-rate
deliveries and follow-through communication
help keep the voyage ascending skyward.*

SUPER SUMMARY
Follow-Through

- Follow through to ensure your customer's satisfaction.
  - Have your customer confirm that no expectation has been left unaddressed or unfulfilled.
  - Deliver in abundance: early, more, better, special.

- Follow through to ensure your sale holds in place.
  - Reassure your prospect he's made the right decision.
    - Congratulate him heartily.
    - Shake hands, where appropriate.
  - Deliver the product or service as rapidly as possible.
  - Follow-up within a few days.
    - Discover and handle any problems quickly and effectively.
    - Give continuous reassurance as needed.

- Follow through to increase opportunities for future sales.
  - During the initial follow-up call, ask satisfied customers for referrals.
  - Continue to keep in excellent communication with your client base.

- Follow up at regular intervals and for special occasions.
- Use some of these opportunities to ask for more referrals.
  - Offer creative incentives and rewards.

9

HANDLING
OBJECTIONS

AND OTHER TROUBLESHOOTING

In Chapter 7, Closing, we took a light look at the subject of *objections* which might come up during the course of a sale.

As this subject of objections and how to handle them is such a vital element to successful selling, I thought we should take another, much closer look.

> **Unhandled objections are the common denominator of nearly all hang-ups which occur during the process of a sale.**

If your prospect balks at any point in the process, you have almost certainly run into an objection, whether your prospect has stated it or not.

UNEXPRESSED OBJECTIONS

It is a VERY common occurrence for a sale to bog down even though no specific objection has been voiced. But if it bogs, you can bet there's an objection there somewhere:

PROSPECT: "Okay. Thanks for the demonstration. It's perfect for me. When I'm ready to buy one, I'll definitely buy it from you."

SALESMAN: "I appreciate that very much. It does seem perfect for you and I'd very much like to see you have it.

"But before you go, tell me, is there some way I could help you to be more ready and perhaps earn your business today?" (Clarify)

PROSPECT: "Well, I like the product, *but my funds won't become available for ten more days.*"

> ***Once you get that objection into view,***
> ***you can begin to work on it.***

Assuming your prospect is potentially ready and able to commit, that your product and company are overall as good as any that can properly fulfill his requirements, and that your terms are fair ones, *a prospect's objections to your moving the sale forward are usually working against his own best interests.*

As we saw earlier, although objections can surface at just about any time and come at you in an almost infinite variety of forms, *there is a very simple, workable way of dealing with any and all of them.*

IT'S ONE OR THE OTHER

Objections fall into one of two categories:

1) Those that can be handled with communication alone; and

2) Those that require an actual, real-world handling.

As we noted in Chapter 7, Closing, it is wisest to try to handle nearly ANY objection with communication alone and

> ***Only resort to real-world solutions when communication alone will not dissolve the objection.***

Before reviewing the actual steps one would take to handle an objection, let's take a quick look at the winning *attitude* a salesperson should have regarding objections.

THE WINNING ATTITUDE

- The Super Salesman attitude regarding handling objections is to *always see yourself and your prospect as "teammates,"* with you as the team leader, joined in a mutual effort to help move the prospect beyond any obstacles which threaten to keep him from acquiring the product or service he needs (and keep you from making a sale).

- View any objection that surfaces as a hitherto hidden barrier, which, now visible, can be dealt with and overcome.

- Whenever the prospect offers you an objection, welcome it as a gift.

- Handle each objection with no less care and skill than it takes to reduce it out of the way of the sale.

HOW TO HANDLE OBJECTIONS—Step by Step

Let's take a detailed look at exactly how to go about handling objections:

Step One—CLARIFY

Whenever a prospect gives you an objection, be sure you understand it EXACTLY or get the prospect to clarify his objection for you until you are sure you do understand it exactly. Otherwise you may be "reading" him wrong and end up handling a nonexistent objection, while leaving his actual objection intact.

WRONG WAY:

PROSPECT: "Is this price firm?"

SALESMAN: "Well, if you think the price is too high I'd be glad to check with the manager."

PROSPECT: "That's what I was afraid of, a place that has wishy-washy prices. I'm out of here."

RIGHT WAY:

PROSPECT: "Is this price firm?"

SALESMAN: "That's an excellent question. *Why do you ask?*" (Clarify)

PROSPECT: "Because I like to do business in places with set prices. I don't like to haggle."

SALESMAN: "Thank you for clarifying that for me. I really appreciate your attitude." (Acknowledgement)

"I can assure you that the price as marked is a very fair one and is the price we ask from anyone who walks through the door." (Handled with Communication)

PROSPECT: "Good policy. I'll take it."

Step Two—ACKNOWLEDGE

One of the biggest mistakes a salesman can make is to *argue* with an objection when it is stated. There are two reasons why this is so:

Firstly, if you are too resistant to your prospect's objections, greeting them harshly or argumentatively, the prospect will feel *punished* rather than *rewarded* for offering up his objection to you and is quite likely to reduce his willingness to work with you further. And secondly,

> ***Doing anything with an objection,***
> ***other than clarifying, understanding and***
> ***acknowledging it, tends to make it persist.***

WRONG WAY:

PROSPECT: "Gosh. That's a little more than I expected to pay for this computer. I've seen similar for less."

SALESMAN: "Well, I don't know what you think you've seen, but if you want a computer with *these* features, that's how much it's going to cost you."

PROSPECT: "NO! I don't think I need to pay that much for a computer. I'm going to keep shopping."

> ***The winning way to greet an objection is***
> ***to acknowledge it with understanding,***
> ***while maintaining as agreeable and***
> ***supportive an attitude as possible.***

RIGHT WAY:

> PROSPECT: "Gosh. That's a little more than I expected to pay for this computer. I've seen similar for less."
>
> SALESMAN: *"I hear what you're saying and I can completely understand* how $2,000 might sound like a lot for this computer." (Acknowledgement)
>
> "With your permission, I'd like to show you more of why this particular computer is such a great value for you at $2,000 . . ." (Handle)

SPECIAL NOTE: There is a fine line and yet an enormous difference between the merits of remaining *agreeable* (as in the example above) and the pitfalls of *going into agreement with an objection*, as in the example below.

> PROSPECT: "Gosh. That's a little more than I expected to pay for this computer. I've seen similar for less."
>
> SALESMAN: "Well, I can show you some cheaper models or maybe some used ones. Or perhaps you'd rather just hold off 'til this model goes on sale."
>
> PROSPECT: "Yes, I'll hold off for now and maybe come back when it's on sale . . . *IF I'm still in the market."*

You want to keep the relationship *agreeable* so that the communication channels remain open enough for you to get the objection dissolved. But you do NOT want to fortify the objection by *agreeing with it!*

You can almost always find *something* about what your prospect has said to agree with, as in the "Right Way" example, at the top of this page, without actually agreeing with and fortifying the objection itself:

> PROSPECT: "Gosh. That's a little more than I expected to pay for this computer. I've seen similar for less."

SALESMAN: "I can completely understand how $2,000 might sound like a lot of money for this computer. . . ."

Acknowledgements Can Dissolve Objections

> "An acknowledgement tends to terminate or end the cycle* of a communication and when expertly used can sometimes stop a continued statement or continued action."[18]
>
> "An acknowledgement is a very, very powerful sixteen-inch gun . . . you should use it to end cycles of communication."[19]
>
> L. Ron Hubbard

A powerful magic often takes place simply by giving your prospect a thorough acknowledgement for communicating his objection to you. It can make that objection *vanish*!

This being the case, a thorough acknowledgement becomes one of your most potent Closing tools.

Always try to make the acknowledgement of your prospect's objection the right intensity and magnitude for what's been said.

To help ensure that your acknowledgement gets experienced *as an acknowledgement*, be sure it is delivered as a distinct and separate communication from anything you say immediately following it.

I cannot overstate the power of a great acknowledgement.

---

* Cycle: Anything which has a beginning, a middle and an end.[20]

> **An excellent acknowledgement alone will often handle a stated objection.**

So, be prepared to discover that your prospect's objection has diminished notably upon your acknowledgement of it—or has vanished altogether.

EXAMPLE:

PROSPECT: "Well, to tell you the truth, I'm just a little hesitant. This is a pretty big decision for me."

SALESMAN: *"Thank you very much for sharing that with me. I know how important a decision this is for you. I really do understand."* (Acknowledgement)

PROSPECT: "Well, heck, now that I've said it . . . I feel a lot more relaxed about this thing . . . (takes two breaths) . . . Okay. Sign me up."

Step Three—DISSOLVE THE OBJECTION WITH COMMUNICATION

While an excellent acknowledgement alone will often get the job done, many, if not most times, more work is required.

Once your prospect has given you his exact objection and an acknowledgement alone hasn't dissolved it, help him to re-evaluate his viewpoint until his objection is no longer blocking him from moving forward.

> **Put the situation into a perspective whereby your prospect would see himself as a winner by moving forward with the sale.**

Use What You Have Learned

It is especially effective, when addressing his objections, to *call up and use what you previously learned about his needs and wants for your product, and the importances he has in his life for acquiring your product.*

EXAMPLE:

SALESMAN: "So, all that's left to do is go ahead and set a date to install the roofing on your house."

PROSPECT: "Not yet. I still feel I owe it to myself to shop your competitors to make absolutely sure that I'm getting the very best possible deal."

SALESMAN: "Thank you for letting me know that. I definitely understand how important it is to get a good deal these days. Just to make sure I'm tracking with you, tell me, what *exactly* do you mean by 'the very best possible deal'?" (Clarify)

PROSPECT: "I mean the *lowest price.*"

SALESMAN: "Of course." (Acknowledgement)

"Well, since we guarantee our price is the lowest available and since, *as you mentioned earlier, the quality of the installation is also extremely important to you,* and, as you know, we have the best reputation in the area, wouldn't you like to just go ahead and get this close-out special now, while we still have these shingles in stock?" (Handle)

Use the Key Motivation

In Chapter 5, "Qualifying," we talked about the very special importance of discovering your prospect's main, core, *single most important reason for needing or wanting your product:* his "Key Motivation."

Using his Key Motivation during your presentation, you will have convincingly shown your prospect how the features of your product or service will satisfy this prime need of his.

As you and your prospect enter the close, however, despite the fact that your prospect has apparently found the product he needs, now, when the tension of making an actual buying commitment is upon him, the prospect can potentially lose his focus.

There are times when a prospect will bring so much sales resistance in on himself that his sense of better judgment becomes clouded and he loses his positive perspective. His attention becomes less and less focused on why he wanted to buy the product and more and more focused onto objections or reasons why *not* to buy the product!

> *Using your prospect's Key Motivation is the most powerful tool you have to get his attention refocused back onto the positive and to get the sale moving forward again.*

Whenever a prospect's own sales resistance beefs up so much that it turns his attitude negative and *seriously* threatens to stand between him and his gaining what he needs and wants, it's time for you, his Super Salesman, to bring out the heavy artillery. It's time for you to use what you know about his Key Motivation to get his attention refocused back onto acquiring the product or service that will enhance his life.

> *Hard sell means insistence that*
> *people buy. It means caring*
> *about the person and not accepting*
> *reasons why it cannot be done,*
> *but caring enough to get him*
> *through the stops or barriers . . .*[21]
>
> L. Ron Hubbard

EXAMPLE:

PROSPECT: "Uh, well . . . this is a big decision . . . I better think it over some more. I'll get back with you in . . . say a month or so."

SALESMAN: "I do understand your hesitance . . ." (Acknowledgement)

"But Bob, you already know that our prices are fair and that our reputation for doing great work and standing behind the work is the best in the area.

"Earlier you told me that *the reason you came in today was that your roof has now deteriorated so badly that last night's rain came right through and watered your INDOOR plants! You told me how one more rain like that will ruin your furniture and floors.*" (his Key Motivation for seeking a roofing solution)

"I know decisions like this one can be difficult, but I promise you, deciding to go ahead with this is the best decision you can make. Let's move forward and get your roof fixed up before the next rain. Now (form in hand) how do you spell your last name?"

PROSPECT: "G-r-a-t-e-f-u-l".

EXAMPLE:

PROSPECT: "No. Not today. I'll just think about it."

SALESMAN: "I can truly understand your reluctance." (Acknowledgement)

"Before you leave, let me ask you something, Jerry. When we were talking earlier, you mentioned that your current computer is so slow, it's interfering with the efficiency of your day-trading. That you don't have the edge you need in a fast moving market. That you suspect it's costing you as much as $1,000 a week in your trades. That if you don't turn that around, you may need to give up day-trading altogether. But that you love day-trading and don't want to give it up. *You told me that the basic reason you want a new, faster computer is to get the edge you need to hold onto day-trading and your life style.*" (his Key Motivation)

"Let's do this. Let's equip you with this faster than lightning, kill-the-competition model. Try trading on this machine for a week. If this doesn't give you the edge you need, take advantage of our seven-day-satisfaction policy and bring it back. If it does—it will more than pay for itself in about three weeks and you'll be where you want to be on your day-trading. You have nothing to lose and a lot to gain. How does that sound to you?"

PROSPECT: "If I can pay for it with a personal check, you have yourself a deal."

EXAMPLE:

PROSPECT: "I understand everything you've explained to me, Doctor, but I think I should wait another paycheck or two before I get the procedure done."

DOCTOR: "I certainly understand your hesitancy, Mary. I really, really do." (Acknowledgement)

"And if holding off a few weeks didn't matter, I'd have no problem with that.

"You and your family have been coming to me with your medical concerns for a long time now. I think you know you can trust me and what I'm about to say to you.

"*You told me that this condition has been worrying you so much, you've been sleepless and irritable to the point it's completely disrupting your life and that was the main reason you came to see me today.*" (her Key Motivation)

"You need this procedure and I want to go ahead and schedule it. I don't want you to worry about the finances. Angela will work out an arrangement with you. Now, do you want to have it done this afternoon or tomorrow morning?"

PROSPECT: "I know you're right, Doctor Michael. Tomorrow morning will be fine . . . And thank you."

Your prospects want and/or need that which you are offering. If they begin to stand in their own way of acquiring it, your single most potent action to bring them back on track toward getting it, is to

> ***Remind them of the single most important reason why they felt they needed your product or service in the first place.***

Remind them of the Key Motivation they told you about earlier in the sales process.

Multiple Objections

Sometimes you'll get one objection handled, only to discover another one sitting right behind it which also needs to be addressed:

PROSPECT: "That makes a lot of sense. Thanks for making me aware of the special price on your siding. I'm convinced to go ahead and get it . . . *but* . . . *first I'll need to see if the wife approves of the color.*"

When a second objection surfaces, you follow the same procedure you did for the first one, and try to handle it with communication alone, moving the sale forward:

SALESMAN: "Well, I can understand that." (Acknowledgement)

"How about if we go ahead with the paperwork and then you can bring a sample over to your wife and surprise her? If by any chance she isn't thrilled with the color, she can come in and we'll help her pick a color that *will* make her happy." (Handle with Communication)

Step Three-A (If Necessary)—HANDLE WITH REAL-WORLD SOLUTIONS

As noted earlier, sometimes, despite the best of your efforts, there remains an objection which will not resolve with communication alone and needs some real-world handling:

> PROSPECT: "Nope. Completely out of the question. My wife would divorce me if I went ahead and actually committed to the siding without her seeing the color first."

When a real-world handling is required, the guiding principles are:

A. Remain solution-oriented.

- Maintain your positive Super Salesman outlook, that "there *is* a way to make this happen and together we are going to find it"; and

- Encourage your prospect to also take the solution viewpoint of "HOW can we overcome this obstacle and complete the sale?"

B. Guide your prospect to come up with a solution or come up with one yourself.

- He probably knows the overall scene much better than you do and is therefore the best person to create the solution. But, if he can't or won't come up with the solution himself, despite your help and guidance, then YOU come up with it.

C. The quicker the solution is found and implemented, the better.

Make It Work

You need to be as clever as you can when creating solutions. Try to get your prospect to, or help your prospect to, come up with the best possible plan which will allow him to buy the product as soon as possible:

SALESMAN: "Well, then, let's get your wife's agreement on the color. What do *you* think is the best, most direct way we could do that?"

PROSPECT: "There really is *no* way we could do it at this point. Why don't I just check back with you in about two or three weeks?"

Keep at It

Don't give up and don't let him give up. If he doesn't come up with a solution himself, you come up with it for him:

SALESMAN: "I hear you." (Acknowledgement)

"Hey! What if you give your wife a call and *invite her to come over to see a sample of the color?* You and I can have a cup of coffee while we wait." (Real-world handle)

PROSPECT: "That would be one heck of a long cup of coffee since my wife is en route to Nova Scotia for an International yodeling competition and won't be back for two weeks! And the sale on the siding will probably be over by then. So, why don't we just forget it?"

SALESMAN: "Yes. You're right." (Acknowledgement)

"The sale on the siding will be over by then . . . But what if I pay for overnight air and *zip the color sample up to her at her hotel?*"

PROSPECT: "That's brilliant. Why didn't I think of that? She'll be all settled in by tomorrow and we could get it to her then."

If I Do It, Will You Do It?

A special word of caution here on addressing an objection with a real-world handling when there may be one or more additional objections lurking behind it:

Before embarking on any *excessively time consuming, strenuous* or *expensive solutions,* it is wise to discover if there is likely to be more than the one objection holding up the sale.

EXAMPLE:

SALESMAN: "So, *if we* overnight-air the sample and your wife likes the color, *is there anything else* that would prevent you from finalizing the paperwork tomorrow evening?"

PROSPECT: "Nope. With her okay, we are 100% ready to roll."

SALESMAN: "Good. Let's send off the sample."

Step Four—MOVE THE SALE FORWARD

Once the objection is handled, proceed forward with the sale. If the objection was one which dissolved with communication alone, move forward *immediately*:

PROSPECT: "That's a big relief to know that this is one of the most reliable units on the market . . . Okay. Sign me up."

SALESMAN: "I know you're going to be happy with that decision, Dave. Would you prefer to pay all cash or finance part of it?"

Schedule Out the Steps

If the solution to an objection requires a real-world handling which stalls the sale from moving forward immediately, schedule out the steps of the solution:

- EXACTLY,
- COMPLETELY, and
- AS TIGHTLY AS POSSIBLE.

EXAMPLE:

SALESMAN: "Okay, so what do you say we meet here tomorrow evening at 6:00 so we can get your wife's call okaying the color and wrap this thing up at that time."

PROSPECT: "I'll be here at 6:00 sharp, checkbook in hand."

When real-world solutions are required, you want to

> *Do everything you appropriately can to move the procedure forward so the sale closes as soon as possible,*

before other factors in life have much of a chance to move in to slow or stop the sale from happening.

These are the exact four steps which will successfully get you through any objection you will ever run into. The only other variable at work here is how creatively and brilliantly you manage to execute the steps.

• • • • •

TO REGAIN CONTROL—ASK A QUESTION

Another potential barrier to getting your prospect successfully through the sales process is your prospect attempting to take over control.

At times, a relatively cooperative prospect will unwittingly begin to lead the sale astray by steering attention off course into a non-productive direction. There are also times when you will have aggressive prospects who actively try to grab away control to run things their own way.

When you run into these phenomena, you need to be able to take back control as fast as you appropriately can.

There's a super simple, two-step formula which will allow you to do just that—a formula based on the principle that:

> ### *He who is directing the attention is in control of the sale.*

A primary key to redirecting the prospect's attention and thereby regaining and retaining control is to:

Be the one asking the questions.

To take control back from a prospect whose statements or questions are misdirecting the sale:

1) Thoroughly *acknowledge* **the prospect's statement or question and**

2) Start asking and getting answers to questions of your own.

And, of course, try to ask questions which lead the attention in the direction you want the sale to go.

EXAMPLE:

PROSPECT: "... and when we aren't playing checkers, me and the family like to take long, LONG, aimless walks through the woods in the back of our house ..."

SALESMAN: (Jumping in when prospect pauses momentarily to take a breath) "You sound like you have quite the family there, Willy." (Acknowledgement)

"*Let me ask you a question.* Is that the same woods you mentioned earlier, that has begun to grow so thick it motivated you to come in today to shop for one of our chainsaws?"

PROSPECT: "Oh! Yeah. That's right! We've gotta thin out those woods big time. We really need one of these chainsaws."

EXAMPLE:

SALESMAN: *(Attempting to Open the sale)* "Good morning. My name is Al. Welcome to Pampered Pre-Owned Autos of Temecula."

PROSPECT: *(Attempting to take over control with a Presentation question)* "Hi, Al. My name is Myron. Nice to meet you. Al, *let me ask you something*, can you show me which one of these cars is the best deal on the lot?"

SALESMAN: "Very good question, Myron." (Acknowledgement).

(*Retaining control by asking a Qualifying question*) "And I'll be glad to point it out to you. But, before I do, *let me ask you a question.* Are you more interested in a two-door coupe or do you need a four-door sedan?"

PROSPECT: "Oh no. No two-door coupes. I want a four-door sedan and it's gotta be either white with tan interior or silver with gray. And it has to have air conditioning and a good CD, but no leather. And it's gotta have automatic transmission and . . ."

EXAMPLE:

PROSPECT: (*Attempting to take over control of the Close with a question*) "So, what's the best price you can give me on this model?"

SALESMAN: "Good question." (Acknowledgement)

(*Keeping control by asking a question*) "Are you actually ready to sit down and close a deal on this boat if we can work out the price for you right now?"

PROSPECT: "No. I still need to think about it. So, if you'll just give me *your* best price, I'll take it with me and see if I can get any other boat yard to beat it by a few bucks. If not, I'll come back to you."

(*Again attempting to take over control of the Close with a question*) "So, what's your best price on this rig?"

SALESMAN: "I completely understand your question and your desire to get the very best price you can on the purchase of your boat, Mr. Locke." (Acknowledgement)

"And I assure you, if you'll give me the opportunity to earn your business, I'll be more than willing to sit down with you and work out a price you'll be very happy with.

"You mentioned that it's very important to you to do business with a company located near your home, as we are, and that with so many boat yards going out of business lately, you want to do business with a company you can count on to back you up well after the sale.

"We wouldn't have been able to stay in business for over 125 years if we didn't treat our customers at LEAST as well as any of our competitors, all of whom, by the way, are located pretty far away from here."

(Keeping control by asking another question) "I know we can work out a price for you that you'll be happy with, and I'd like the opportunity to sit down with you right now and earn your business. What do we need to do to earn it?"

PROSPECT: "Well. You're definitely the closest and have a great reputation . . . Okay . . . If you can work out a deal that includes the towing kit and the extended warranty, and promise to deliver in under two weeks, I'm ready to sit down and talk turkey."

SALESMAN: "Please have a seat . . ."

If you want to get back in control and stay there: Acknowledge the prospect's questions or statements and start asking and getting answers to questions of your own.

We'll look at some additional uses of this Asking-a-Question technique in the upcoming chapter, "It's Out of Order."

MORE SECOND OPINIONS—Use Outside Experts

In the chapter on Closing, we looked at the advantage of using both enthusiastic customers and your fellow workers to help give certain of your prospects the reassurance they might need in order to make their commitment to buy.

You will find that just as the affirming opinions of other customers and co-workers can help handle prospects that need that extra assurance, sometimes an opinion from an *outside expert* confirming your closing data can be similarly influential in giving such prospects the extra reassurance they may need to go ahead and commit.

So, another way to effectively use "Second Opinions" is to

> *Make sure you have experts lined up and available who can help you handle the most common objections that you frequently find you are running into.*

The expert might be a technician or perhaps a financial or legal expert—all depending upon the nature of your product and the sort of objection you ordinarily find yourself having to deal with.

If, for example, you were trying to close a real estate investment deal, you might call upon a reputable appraiser for a second opinion to handle an objection regarding the property's value; or an attorney familiar with your business to affirm that your proposition is a completely legitimate one; or a good mortgage broker to reassure your prospect that the terms are favorable; or an accountant to confirm the tax advantages of the deal.

You would simply line up an expert or two, who you would prearrange to be called upon when a particular objection arose that pertained to his area of expertise.

EXAMPLE:

PROSPECT: "Well, Bob, I've decided on this tractor alright, but I'm not going to say yes until I double check just how reliable I can expect this model to be."

SALESMAN: "I hear you. Reliability is definitely an important consideration." (Acknowledgement)

"Let me ask you something, Dave. Would you take the word of the head mechanic over at the Greenville Motor Rebuilding Plant on the reliability of this model?"

PROSPECT: "You bet I would. If *he* says it's reliable, you have yourself a deal."

SALESMAN: "Well, let's get him on the phone and get you into this tractor."

The more reputable and trustworthy the expert, the better.

TEAM ASSIST

There are occasions when you may run out of ideas on how to handle a prospect's objection or just plain *don't know what else to do* to keep a particular sale moving forward. Rather than letting the prospect end off or having the sale stall out, the best way to save that sale is often to

> ### *Invite one of your sales team members in to assist.*

This technique is especially handy while you are still training up on sales techniques or on a particular product line. In addition to helping you save your sale, getting to observe a more experienced or more knowledgeable teammate in action can also help you increase your own knowledge and expertise.

You'll find it a smart policy to always have a seasoned team member—whether a fellow salesperson or a sales manager—standing by for a possible "Team Assist."

In using this technique, you're not simply seeking a "Second Opinion" from a co-worker. With a Team Assist, you would actually *turn over control* of the prospect and of the sale to a helpful teammate. The turn-over may take place right where you and your prospect are working together or you may choose to escort the prospect to where the teammate is located for turning over.

The Team Assist can be a partial handling, in which the teammate gets the sale moving forward again and then returns control of the prospect back to you for completing the sale, or it can end up with the teammate retaining control and fully closing the sale himself.

Each situation has its own set of circumstances which will determine which of these two options is the best choice for any particular sale. All things being equal, I heavily recommend that control of the prospect be passed back to the original salesperson for completing the sale. It's usually the original salesperson who has spent the most time with the prospect, developed the deeper relationship with him and knows more about the prospect and his specific needs and wants. So, if it would not jeopardize the close by passing control back to the original salesperson, it is almost always the preferable choice.

In turning over a prospect, always try to:

- Bring the teammate in as smoothly and logically as possible;

- Give all vital Qualifying and Closing data over to your teammate in the presence of your prospect;

- Have your prospect confirm the validity of the data (This serves as a reality check for all present.);

- Stay present while your teammate proceeds with your prospect (Not only can you learn from it, but it also keeps you abreast of all that transpires—which you may need to know to properly complete the sale if you end up back in the process.);

- Once you've turned it over, remain as tight-lipped as possible, so as not to undermine your teammate's control of the procedure; and

- Unless you observe a vital need to pull the prospect back, leave it up to your teammate to decide if he will keep and close the sale or return the prospect to you.

EXAMPLE:

PROSPECT: "I really appreciate your trying so hard, Bob, but unless you can think of a more creative way I can finance this tractor, I'll say good-bye for now and get back to you when I get it figured out."

SALESMAN: "I hear you, Dave." (Acknowledgement)

"Hold on a minute. I know you really need that tractor. If there is anyone who would know if there's a way to create a financing solution, it's Lowell Ganzer. Come with me." (marches into sales manager's office, confident the prospect is right behind him) "Lowell, this is Dave." (Sales manager shakes prospect's hand)

"Dave needs to replace his tractor before next month's harvest or his crop could be ruined. He's decided on the 'Big Momma' model and the only hold-up is the financing. We've exhausted all the conventional routes and come up dry. If we can figure out how to get the financing, Dave is ready to sign the purchase agreement and give us his 10% down payment right now." (Confronting Dave eye-to-eye) "Isn't that right, Dave?"

PROSPECT: "Yep. You show me how I can get the financing and I'm ready."

SLS MNGR: (Looking over the application form brought in by the salesman) "Well, I see here you're an Armed Forces Veteran, Dave."

PROSPECT: "Yep."

SLS MNGR: "Take a look at this announcement." (Handing a document over to the prospect)

"As a Veteran, you are *automatically qualified* for the Government Farm Subsidy Loan Program, entitling you to 90% financing at 1% below the market rates on farm equipment such as the Big Momma."

PROSPECT: "Wow! This is GREAT."

SLS MNGR: "Bob, why don't you have Dave sit down in your office and fill out this loan form. And then, while the two of you are finalizing the down payment and purchase agreement, I'll have the loan form fired off to the Veterans Administration and we should have this whole thing wrapped up in a flash."

SALESMAN: (Taking form from sales manager) "Thanks, Lowell. Dave, follow me and we'll get you all fixed up."

PROSPECT: "You bet I will." (As they return to salesman's office) "And Bob, thank you for getting the help we needed instead of giving up on me."

When you run out of ideas on how to handle an objection or you just don't know what to do next, rather than letting a sale stall out, get a Team Assist.

NOTE: A "Team Assist" is a prospect-friendly technique in which a salesperson, who would ordinarily see the sale through to its completion, runs into a situation which seems to require the assistance of a team member to keep the sale moving forward. And so he attempts to unstick a stuck sales process by seeking the good help of a competent, trusted teammate.

This is not to be confused with the conventional technique of "Turn Over" (or "T.O.")—which is a way of selling whereby you have one salesperson Open, Qualify and Present to the prospect and then have a second salesperson step in, often abruptly, to Close the sale. In that system, the initial salesperson is usually the more appealing, milder of the two. Once the prospect is "primed" by this first, friendly fellow, in comes the "Closer," who is usually a formidable, forceful and authoritative person, armed with techniques designed to push, pull, trick or over-whelm the prospect into a commitment.

If you have successfully managed to *penetrate*—winning your prospect's trust; discovering his needs and wants; convincingly demonstrating to him how your product will adequately satisfy these needs and wants; and you are willing and able to guide him past the stops and barriers of his own sales resistance—you will not need to resort to trickery or overwhelm to get your prospect to commit.

BACK-OUT ATTEMPTS

On occasion, you will have a prospect who will have "Buyer's Remorse" for one reason or another and attempt to renege on his commitment or want to refund his purchase.

> ### *The handling for attempted back-out is the same as for any other objection.*

You simply:

1) Get him to clarify what he wishes to do and why he wishes to do it until you understand it completely;

2) Acknowledge it agreeably, supportively and thoroughly;

3) Handle his objection(s); and

4) "Re-close" him on his decision to buy.

WRONG WAY:

CUSTOMER: "Hey, Bill, we're going to have to cancel the contract on the house."

SALESMAN: "Cancel?! @#%! Just what I was afraid of. Look, Don, I've put six months of effort into finding you and Maureen that little two-bedroom cottage.

"I could have been spending my time helping other people who could afford bigger houses and earned myself some really nice commissions instead of fooling around with the two of you.

"And now you're telling me I'm going to lose the measly commission I would have made if you would have stuck to your word and not tried to weasel out of this?!"

CUSTOMER: "Are you done, Bill?"

SALESMAN: "Yeah. You bet I am."

CUSTOMER: "Well, Bill, I think you should know that the reason we're canceling is that Maureen just learned of an inheritance she'll be getting in a few weeks and we are going to be moving up to the kind of splendid home we've always dreamed of. We very much appreciated how hard you worked for us and how patient you had been with us. I was going to ask you to start looking for that dream house for us. But you know what, Bill, I no longer think you're the kind of person we want to do business with."

No matter how much effort you've put into the sale and no matter how tempted you may be to snap at your prospect when he tells you he intends to undo the sale, it is very important to resist all temptation to react in a hostile or antagonistic manner toward him.

Despite the element of threat, the wisest course of action is to keep your Super Salesman hat on as straight as ever and handle the announcement properly and professionally, as you would any other objection he brings to your attention.

Once you are clear on exactly why he wishes to cancel, and you've thoroughly acknowledged what he had to say, you can then proceed to handle the situation at whatever level of firmness is appropriate for the circumstances.

RIGHT WAY:

CUSTOMER: "Bob, I'm sorry to have to tell you this, but I am going to have to cancel the order for the tractor."

SALESMAN: "I see. What, exactly, is your situation, Dave?"

CUSTOMER: "We're just in an unexpected tight spot. We thought we had the government loan money coming in next month, which would have covered the financing, but it fell through."

SALESMAN: "Wow! I'm sure that wasn't easy news for you to have received. I'm very sorry to hear that. I like you, Dave, and care about you and if there is anything I can do to help you out, I'd like to try and do it. Have they canceled out totally?"

CUSTOMER: "Oh, no. They just dropped us out of the program for this quarter and won't be coming through for another three months or so."

SALESMAN: "Oh. Well at least it'll be coming a little ways down the line. Listen, Dave, I know you need that tractor. If we could arrange to defer the billing for three or four months, would you want to go ahead with the purchase?"

CUSTOMER: "Bob, if you can manage to do that for us, you'll have earned yourself a customer for life."

HOW TO TURN "NO, NO, NO" ... INTO ... "YES, YES, YES"

One of the toughest things a salesman faces is what to do when his prospect says "No."

Schools of salesmanship routinely tell you, "Don't take 'NO' for an answer." Some say don't take "No" the first time he says it, but if he says it a second time, end off there. Others say not to accept it until a prospect has said it three or more times, and still others say not to take "No" for an answer at all.

But how do you go past "No" even *once* without damaging your relationship with your prospect and ruining the sale?

Many salespeople, uncertain what to do when faced with a prospect saying "No," simply accept that first "No" as the answer and stop trying to make the sale:

WRONG WAY:

SALESMAN: "So, Mr. Tuffy, will that be check or credit card?"

PROSPECT: "That will be neither, son. *I won't be buying it today at all.*"

SALESMAN: "Okay. No problem. Here's my business card and whenever you're ready, please give me a call."

While it is nearly never a good idea to phrase a closing question in such a way that your prospect could possibly answer with a "No," there are times, such as in the example above, when no matter how you phrase your question, your prospect will tell you that he does not intend to buy.

The Single Greatest Secret to Consistent Closes

> *All a salesman has to do is continue to try to interest the customer and the customer will come through his stages of resistance and will eventually become interested.*[22]
>
> Based on the works of L. Ron Hubbard

In these last several chapters, we've gone over a lot of rules and guidelines on how to successfully work your way up to and through the close. Nestled among them are two principles, which when properly combined together, form a powerhouse duo for consistent selling success. The dynamic pairing of these two principles is the very blueprint of how to turn "No, No, No" into "Yes, Yes, Yes."

In Chapter 7, "Closing," and again in this chapter, we went over the extraordinary ability an excellent *acknowledgement* can have to deflate a prospect's objection.

And we have similarly, in this chapter as well as in earlier chapters, looked at the necessity of *being persistent* in your efforts to continuously move the sales process forward.

When you are trying to close your sale, there is no more reliable combination of ingredients to assure the success of your close than to:

> *Thoroughly acknowledge each objection as it comes up, AND continue to try to interest the prospect until you either hit his next objection or until your prospect becomes interested enough to say "Yes" and the sale closes.*

You just continue this process of acknowledging his reasons "why not," no matter how many objections he brings up, no matter how many times he says "No." You persist forward, continuing to interest him in your product, until your prospect's objections have been sufficiently deflated by your acknowledgements, and his interest in your product has been sufficiently built up for you to close the sale.

If in the process, you hit an objection that won't reduce out of the way with acknowledgement alone, then handle it with "communication only," if possible, or with "real-world handling," if necessary, all the while continuing to try to interest the prospect in your product.

A word of encouragement here: *Please don't let your concern or fear that this procedure might offend or upset your prospect keep you from using it.*

An excellent acknowledgment, in addition to taking the wind out of your prospect's objections, also acts to *soothe* the communication line between you and your prospect. An excellent acknowledgement acts as a buffer, minimizing the prospect's urge or need to feel opposed, upset or antagonized. This additional benefit of the acknowledgement opens the door wide for you to go past "No" over and over again, without jeopardizing the workability of the relationship.

Removing the Thorn from the Prospect's Paw

This does not mean to say that a prospect will not become at all antagonistic during the procedure.

As his failed efforts to resist the sales process set in on him, the prospect may, in one way or another, try to inhibit the sale from proceeding. This is especially true in the early stages of the process. When that fails, the prospect may attempt to exert some force to try to counter the salesman's forward efforts.

During these stages of sales resistance, you may indeed encounter a prospect being antagonistic. But, *know* that these attempts of his are merely stages of resistance he is going through on his way to gaining a desire for and interest in your product.

Just continue to try to interest your prospect in your product, despite any and all sales resistance you run into, thoroughly acknowledging his objections as you go, and you *will* get your prospect through his stages of resistance and into a state of desiring your product and being interested in acquiring it.*

RIGHT WAY:

SALESMAN: "So, Mr. Tuffy, will that be check or credit card?"

PROSPECT: "That'll be neither, son. **I won't be buying it** today at all."

SALESMAN: "Okay, Mr. Tuffy. Not a problem." (Acknowledgement)

"If you don't mind me asking, what more do you feel would have to happen before deciding to buy?"

PROSPECT: "**I'm not convinced** this model is the best one on the market for meeting my specifications."

SALESMAN: "Thank you for sharing that concern with me." (Acknowledgement)

---

* The prospect's movement from efforts to *inhibit*, through efforts to *enforce*, until the prospect begins to *desire* the product, followed by strong *interest* in the product, is a concept based upon a scale contained in L. Ron Hubbard's article, D.E.I. [Desire, Enforce, Inhibit] EXPANDED SCALE. [23]

"Please take a look at this Internet page which compares our model to all the competitive models in all the categories that you've expressed concern about."

(Some minutes later)

"I think you can agree with me that our model will satisfy your specifications better than any other out there."

PROSPECT: "Yep. Looks like it would. But **I'm still not going to buy it** from you today."

SALESMAN: "Okay. I understand." (Acknowledgement)

"May I ask you, though, why you consider it would be better to not buy it today?"

PROSPECT: "Yeah. I'll tell you why. I've decided that I definitely want it in Midnight Blue and **you don't have it available** in Midnight Blue."

SALESMAN: "Yes. I remember you mentioned Midnight Blue was one of your favorite colors. Thank you for reminding me." (Acknowledgement)

"Let's take a quick look at this morning's read-out to see if any of our other locations have it available in Midnight Blue."

(A short time later)

"Yep. Here it is in Midnight Blue. I can make a quick call and have it here for you before we finish the paperwork."

PROSPECT: "Well, that's impressive all right, but . . . **No.** Don't bother to make the call. **I'm really not ready to buy** it. I need to think about this some more."

SALESMAN: "Okay. That's fine. I can understand that you may have one or more things about this transaction that you still want to think about." (Acknowledgement)

"What, specifically, may I ask, is it that you still have attention on that may be leaving you reluctant to buy?"

PROSPECT: "No. It's nothing specific . . . well . . . yes it is. The warranty on your model is only 5 years and the number one competitor's model has a 10-year warranty on it. So **I'm not about to jump in and buy** yours."

SALESMAN: "Thank you for being willing to let me know about that concern." (Acknowledgement)

"As you can see from this magazine article, our model is one of the most reliable on the market, rated well above theirs. As a matter of fact, if you read this highlighted section, you'll see that theirs also had a 5-year warranty until recently, but the article explains that when sales fell off due to reliability problems, they found they needed to increase the coverage to 10 years to regain the public's trust.

"We, on the other hand, have maintained our quality right along, and have never lost the public's trust . . . and even with that, if you'd feel more comfortable with a 10-year warranty, I can arrange an extension from our standard 5-year to our deluxe 10-year coverage."

PROSPECT: "Wow. That shines a whole new light on the subject . . . but . . . **I still don't want to buy** today and I'm running out of time and am going to say good-bye for now."

SALESMAN: "Okay, then. Good-bye, Mr. Tuffy. (while shaking hands) Thanks for giving me this opportunity to talk with you today." (Acknowledgement)

"But . . . before you leave, will you tell me what I could have done to have earned your business today?"

PROSPECT: "Well, son, **you *COULDN'T* have earned it** today! I'm gonna shop around and satisfy myself that I'm getting the lowest price. And *that's* where I'm going to be doing business."

SALESMAN: "I certainly understand you wanting to be sure you're getting the lowest price." (Acknowledgement)

"But, you know what, Mr. Tuffy? I think I can save you a lot of valuable shopping time. If you'll go ahead and make your purchase now, I'll give you a written guarantee that your purchase price will be the lowest available in the marketplace and I'll stand behind that guarantee for a full 30 days."

PROSPECT: "I like that. I like that a LOT. And I'm tempted to take you up on it . . . but I've run out of time and I still have some concerns, so **the answer is still "No."**

SALESMAN: (Again, shaking hands good-bye) "I know you're short of time and I appreciate how much of it you've been willing to spend with me this afternoon. And if you still have concerns, I understand how you wouldn't want to conclude your deal." (Acknowledgement)

(Walking alongside the prospect on the way to prospect's car)

"Would you be kind enough to tell me what concerns you still have?"

PROSPECT: "Remember I told you how important it was to me to get top-quality follow-up service? Well, I overheard that fellow in your service department saying how he had just read that the quality of your service area has been consistently 'dropping' compared to your competition. And that's the maker-breaker point for me. So **my answer is still no**."

SALESMAN: (Approaching the prospect's parked car) "Mr. Tuffy, I really appreciate you sharing that particular concern with me. And yes, I do remember you telling me how important follow-up care was to you. And I wouldn't expect you to do business with a company whose service was 'dropping.'" (Acknowledgement)

"I think you'd be very interested to know that what that customer you overheard was referring to was the headline in the business section of today's paper, which reads that our service has been consistently '*TOPPING*,' not 'dropping,' the quality of service of our competition. Our reputation for top-notch service remains intact and I can promise you that you'll get the very best of care if you decide to do business with us. Now, how about joining the winning team and letting me earn your business today?"

PROSPECT: "Well, son, I don't quite know what to say. At this point, I believe I would have gone ahead and completed the deal, but, quite honestly, **I had NO intention of actually buying today** and didn't even bring my checkbook with me."

SALESMAN: "I appreciate your honesty." (Acknowledgement)

"It'll only take a few short minutes to complete the paperwork and I'll be more than happy to follow you back to your office when we're done and you can hand me the check then."

PROSPECT: "Son, you are one persistent man. . . . You've got yourself a deal!"

In the example above, the prospect said "No" **11** times before his persistent salesperson got him to say "Yes"!

This combination of thoroughly acknowledging the objection, and then persisting forward, continuing to try to interest the prospect in your product or service, until your prospect runs out of objections, is the most unstoppable duo in the game of selling.

The salesman and the prospect form a "team" with a mutual objective: To have the prospect acquire the product or service from the salesman which will fulfill the prospect's needs and wants. The road to Super Salesmanship is caringly paved with the effective handling of each and every objection that stands between the team and their mutual goal.

SUPER SUMMARY

Handling Objections and
Other Troubleshooting

- Unhandled objections are the common denominator of nearly all hang-ups in a sale.

- If a sale bogs down, get the objection and handle it.
  - Welcome the statement of an objection as a valuable gift.
  - Handle objections with care, understanding and skill.

- Handle objections with the simple four-step system:

  1) Get it *clarified* as needed.

  2) *Acknowledge* the objection as agreeably and supportively as possible.
     - Remain agree*able* but do not "go-into-agreement-with" the objection.
     - An excellent acknowledgement in itself may cause the objection to vanish. If not:

  3) Dissolve the objection *with communication alone.*
     - Help him to see himself as a winner by proceeding with the sale.
     - Use second opinions to fortify the viewpoint that a decision to buy is the correct decision.

more. . .

- Use what you've learned earlier about his needs and wants to help him overcome his objection.

- Use his Key Motivation to get his attention off of his "why nots" and back onto the "why" he needs and wants to go forward.

3a) Where communication alone won't resolve the objection, handle with *real-world* solutions.

- Remain solution-oriented.

- The quicker the solution is found and implemented, the better.

- Guide the prospect to come up with a solution or come up with one yourself.

- Get your prospect's commitment that once the objection is handled, he will proceed with the sale.

- Schedule out the solution steps exactly, completely, and as tightly as possible, and make sure they happen on schedule.

4) Move the sale forward to completion.

- Handle any new objections that may subsequently surface with this same four-step system.

- *Persist, persist, persist*; clarifying, acknowledging and handling until each objection is reduced out of the way of the sale and the prospect has developed strong enough interest to complete the sale.

- Consider a back-out attempt as just another objection. Handle it with a positive attitude and the same four-step system.

- To take back control, ask a question.

- Turn to teammates for assistance, when needed.

10

"Confusions, no matter how big and formidable they may seem, are composed of data or factors or particles. They have pieces. Grasp one piece and locate it thoroughly. Then see how the others function in relation to it and you have steadied the confusion and, relating other things to what you have grasped, you will soon have mastered the confusion in its entirety." [24]

—L. Ron Hubbard

IT'S OUT OF ORDER

As we have seen, a sale logically moves through a five-step sequence: 1) Prospecting, 2) Opening, 3) Qualifying, 4) Presenting, and 5) Closing.

But, like every other principle in existence, there always seem to be exceptions to the rule.

Prospects sometimes have their own ideas about and influence upon "how the sale is supposed to go"!

As we noted in the last chapter, a prospect may not obligingly conform to this exact order or sequence during any given sales cycle.

TIME TRAVELER

At any given moment, a prospect may surprise his salesman by introducing a brand new piece of unexpected data, or he may have a sudden and unpredicted reaction to a salesman's communication or technique, sending the sale reeling into a step *earlier* or *later* than the step the salesman meant for them to be on, potentially throwing the salesman and his sale into a state of confusion.

EXAMPLE:

The salesman is *prospecting* with,

"Hi. Have you ever heard of Brand X widgets?"

And the prospect catapults the two of them into a *close* with,

"Yes. I've dreamed of owning one for years. A Brand X widget would be the answer to my prayers. Where do I sign and how soon can you deliver it?"

EXAMPLE:

The salesman attempts to *close* with,

"So, will that be cash, check or credit card?"

And the prospect asks,

"Is there a fourth choice? Because my accountant just called and told me I'm insolvent, bankrupt and really quite broke."

plunging the two of them backward into the *qualifying* step.

The more familiar a salesperson is with the characteristics of each of the five steps:

- The quicker he will be to recognize that his prospect is no longer located on the same step of the sale as he is; and
- The more able he will be to effectively handle these "out-of-order" phenomena when they occur.

By Plan or by Punt

So, what do you do when you experience the confusion of being located on a different step of the sale than your prospect is on?

There are times you will simply recognize what is going on and know exactly what to do about it. For all the other times, use the guidelines and procedures laid out in this chapter, and all the wits you can muster, to get both your feet onto solid ground and the sale marching forward again.

KEEP "A WATCHFUL EAR" OPEN FOR NEW INFO

Perhaps the most common out-of-order occurrence is that of fresh qualifying data coming in, which necessitates reevaluation and modification of your in-progress presentation or close. And you'll find that your prospects will *regularly* introduce such additional data about their needs, wants and limitations as you move the sales process forward.

It is the wise salesperson who is vigilant in listening for any additional relevant data and who readily and willingly modifies his presentation and his close to appropriately accommodate and utilize such fresh information.

EXAMPLE:

PROSPECT: "This house you're showing me is lovely but I've just realized something very important. I'll definitely need *three* bathrooms."

SALESMAN: "Okay. Not a problem." (Acknowledgement)

"Let me restudy the listings for homes that have *three* bathrooms, that also meet the rest of your requirements, and I'll get back to you tomorrow."

FULL SPEED AHEAD

There are instances in which a prospect is ready for and appropriately forwards himself onto a later step than the one the salesman thinks they are supposed to be on.

For example, the salesman simply says "Hi" and the prospect opens instantly and begins blurting out his most needed and wanted requirements without the salesman asking a single qualifying question. Or perhaps the prospect begins to present the product *to himself*, or even closes himself on it:

SALESMAN: "Hi, my name is John."

PROSPECT: "Hi, John. I need a hairpiece that will cover my bald spot and make me look real macho and get the ladies totally swooning over me. How about that curly black job over there? Yeah, I like it. I'll take it. Wrap it up."

It is a fairly common phenomenon that while you are still on one of the early stages of the sale, the prospect offers you a "closing signal," a sign that he has made a decision and is ready to buy your product or service.

Perhaps he has done his homework and shopped long and hard before ever entering (or calling) your place of business, and is ripe and ready by the time you first talk to him. Or maybe he's just an impulsive person by nature.

In any case, as we've studied earlier, *whenever you receive a signal that your prospect is ready to commit, cease all other activity and go directly into the close.*

EXAMPLE:

SALESMAN: "Let me put your attention on this unusual piece over here in the corner."

PROSPECT: "Oh, my God! That is the most beautiful example of a Ming vase I have ever laid my eyes upon. I must have it. I've got to have it this very minute."

SALESMAN: *"And so you shall. Would you prefer to use a business check or a personal check?"*

These are examples of a prospect's *acceptable* attempts to move the sale forward. A salesperson would be wise indeed to

> ***Treat acceptable attempts to move the sale forward as a fortuitous piece of luck and go with them.***

PULL IN THOSE REINS

You will, however, also run into times when your prospect will *inappropriately* attempt to move the process forward.

EXAMPLE:

Salesman proceeds to open the sale and his prospect prematurely attempts to fast-forward them into the presentation:

SALESMAN: "Hi. My name is Friendly Freddy. Welcome to Motor Homes of Monterey Hills."

PROSPECT: "Well, Friendly Freddie, you seem like a fellow I can deal with. My name is Joe and I'd like you to tell me everything you know about . . . oh, let's say that big green job over there at the end of the lot."

Here the prospect, having not yet revealed *any* data regarding his needs or wants for the product, is attempting to prematurely move the salesman into the presentation phase of the sale. For the presentation to be highly relevant to the prospect, the salesperson must first discover at least some of the vital qualifying data as to the prospect's needs, wants and limitations.

At times like these,

> **When your prospect attempts to move the process forward prematurely, you should, as smoothly as possible, retain control and keep the sales process running in its proper sequence:**

SALESMAN: "I'll be more than happy to give you all the information you like on that 'big green job over there,' Joe. If you'll allow me, though, *I'd like to first ask you a few questions* to make sure that unit is actually the best one we have for you. Now, were you hoping for a recreational vehicle that sleeps more or less than four? . . ."

EXAMPLE:

Salesman attempts to go into a presentation and the prospect —without offering a Closing Signal—tries to jump them into price negotiation, which properly belongs at the close:

SALESMAN: "Let me present this model to you."

PROSPECT: "What's the best price you can offer me on that model?"

SALESMAN: "Look, Tom, I really can understand your having attention on the price." (Acknowledgement)

"And I'll be more than willing to sit down with you and work out an attractive deal for you. If you will permit me, though, I'd like to first make sure we have *the* model that will best meet your needs before taking up your time, working out the different ways we'd be able to help make a purchase affordable and attractive for you. Now, does this size actually work for you or should we be looking at a larger model?"

NOTE: A salesman's sense of which prospect attempts to move the sale forward are appropriate and which are not appropriate tends to sharpen with experience.

> *If, at any time, you are unclear whether a prospect's attempt to move forward is appropriate or inappropriate, you can always ask the prospect for more data before deciding on which course of action to take.*

EXAMPLE:

PROSPECT: "Excuse me Mr. Salesman. Do you have time to put down your cup of coffee and sell me that new green unit at the end of the lot?"

SALESMAN: "I'd be glad to. *Are you familiar with that model?*"

PROSPECT: "Yep. I owned one almost exactly like it, which got stolen. I came by last night after hours and looked it over stem to stern. It's exactly what I want and the price looks fair. My insurance check came in this morning and I'm ready to sign on the dotted line and drive it away."

SALESMAN: "Then, let me not delay you another moment. Please have a seat at this desk. We'll get you signed right up and on your way!"

ASK A QUESTION

Asking-a-Question of your prospect, as in the example above, is not only an excellent way to clarify the appropriateness of your prospect's attempt to move your sale forward. This technique of Asking-a-Question, as noted in the last chapter, can also be used to regain control of the sale from any prospect who is attempting to lead the sale astray. And that's not all!

Asking-a-Question is one of the most useful, all-purpose sales tools I've ever come across and can be used as a stabilizing solution for just about any situation you might ever run into.

> ***At any point in the sales process you find yourself confused, or just uncertain what exactly to do next, ASK-A-QUESTION.***

This technique, as simple a tool as it is, will help get you out of almost *any* situation.

Asking-a-Question:

* Immediately puts you back in control;
* Gets the prospect to give you additional data, which in itself might prove useful in solving your situation; and
* Buys you some time.

While the prospect is answering the question you've asked him, you can be devoting part of your attention to reevaluating the situation to figure out what the heck is going on and where to go to from there.

This does not have to be the least bit complicated or require much thinking at all.

EXAMPLE:

PROSPECT: "How much is it?"

SALESMAN: "Good question." (Acknowledgement)

"How much were you hoping it would be?"

PROSPECT: "Oh. Well, let me put it like this. I'm on a tight budget this month and so for this to work for me, I need to stay under $800 . . ."

EXAMPLE:

PROSPECT: "Does it come in orange?"

SALESMAN: "That's a good question."(Acknowledgement)

"Is orange the color you need it to be?"

PROSPECT: "Well, no. It doesn't have to be orange, but that would be our number one choice . . . although, if it were a dark yellow or light red . . ."

EXAMPLE:

PROSPECT: "Does it come with the double, sideways, round-about feature?"

SALESMAN: (Unsure what the prospect is talking about) "Very good question!" (Acknowledgement)

"What is it about that feature that you value the most?"

PROSPECT: "Well, I want to be able to sew zigzags in parallel as well as circles within circles."

SALESMAN: (Newly enlightened) "I see. I see." (Acknowledgement)

"This model over here comes with that feature. Here, let me show you . . ."

EXAMPLE:

DESIGNER: "So, how about commissioning me to start designing your website early next week."

PROSPECT: "Well, no. Let's hold off. I'm not sure I want to use you."

DESIGNER: (Thrown aback by prospect's response) "Okay. Not a problem." (Acknowledgement)

"So, let me ask you—*What is it you feel you need that I might not fulfill for you?*"

PROSPECT: "Well . . . ah . . . I'm not convinced you can produce the quality I need in the style I want. I believe you're competent, all right, but I'm not convinced you have enough expertise working with computer animation."

DESIGNER: (Now aware of the objection and having had a bit of time to compose his thoughts) "Fair enough." (Acknowledgement)

"Please let me take another few seconds of your time to show you some sites I've already created using computer animation." (Shows prospective client a couple of eye-popping samples)

PROSPECT: "Yes! That one! That's the exact feel I'm looking for. Okay! Let's talk turkey. Is there any way I could get you to start earlier than next week?"

EXAMPLE:

SALESMAN: (Asking a Trial Closing question) "Were you planning to finance?"

PROSPECT: (Attempting to take control with a question of his own) "What's the lowest, best price you can sell it to me for?"

SALESMAN: "That's a fair question." (Acknowledgement)

(Taking control back with a question)

"If I can offer you an attractive price, are you ready to seal the deal?"

PROSPECT: "If you can take $1,000 down now and give me 30 days to come up with another $1,000 down and finance the balance for payments under $500 a month, I'm ready to sign."

SALESMAN: "There might be a way to work that out." (Acknowledgement)

(Working out figures on a calculator while confirming the commitment)

"So, if I can work this out for $1,000 down now and another $1,000 in 30 days and payments under $500, you'll close the deal right now?"

PROSPECT: "I definitely will. Here's my checkbook right here."

SALESMAN: (Completing his calculation, looking up with a smile and extending his arm for a handshake) "You've got yourself a deal."

You can almost never suffer from Asking-a-Question. And when you find yourself suddenly out of control of the sale or no longer certain how to proceed, Asking-a-Question is the simplest and best handle I know of to get the sale back on track.

WAS IT SOMETHING I SAID?

The other side of the coin from the prospect attempting to move the process *forward*, is his attempt to move it *backward*. You'll run into that, too.

There may be times, for example, that you are qualifying or presenting or closing and you discover that somehow communication has broken down and your prospect is no longer willing to communicate with you openly (if he ever was).

EXAMPLE:

SALESMAN: "So, does our repiping proposal seem like it might work for you, Mr. Cartooni?"

PROSPECT: "No, George, it doesn't. I need to think about it some more."

SALESMAN: "I follow you. Not a problem. But tell me something, Mr. Cartooni, is there anything about our service that seems unsuitable?"

PROSPECT: "No, George. There's something about you that seems unsuitable. My name is *CARTINI*, NOT **CARTOONI !** I've been patient up 'til now, but you've been calling me 'Mr. *Cartooni*' all afternoon and I can't stand it any longer!

"I don't think you and I are going to be able to do business together."

When you discover that the prospect requires more work on an *earlier* step of the sale than the one you considered the two of you were on (in this case, getting back into open communication), you should, as smoothly as possible:

1) Locate *which* earlier step it is that is incomplete;

2) Return to *that* earliest incomplete step;

3) Complete that step; and

4) Move forward to complete the sale.

EXAMPLE:

SALESMAN: "I sincerely beg your pardon, Mr. Cartini, and thank you very much for bringing that to my attention. I have a slight hearing problem and the shop is unusually noisy today. I guess I didn't hear you clearly when you told me your name.

"I really appreciate your being willing to tell me what was bothering you and I can understand your being upset about it. But if you are willing to work with me a bit longer, Mr. Cartini, I'd be happy to address any questions or concerns you have about our repiping service so we can help you solve those plumbing problems."

GROUP PRESENTATION SALES

Another example of out-of-order is a special case, such as in group seminars and other "group presentation sales," in which all the prospects who show up *receive a general presentation before much, if any, one-on-one qualifying has taken place.*

Examples of this would be your free or low-cost, heavily promoted seminars, often held at hotels, to introduce a large public to a service, such as training, consulting or perhaps a multi-level-marketing or other income-producing opportunity.

In the better, more effective group presentation sales, you'll discover that the sponsors have done their homework. Though they have not done a standard qualifying step, they have researched out, identified and included into their presentation that particular audience's "buttons"—those things which, if mentioned in the presentation, are likely to strike an accord and elicit an interest in the product or service being presented:

> " . . .with very little cash investment to get started, with NO selling required, and with the best, simplest training and most active support team in the industry backing you up, we'll show you how to smoothly build your organization, help get this century's best high tech solution distributed to folks who really need and want it, make yourself a mountain of money, have a lot of fun as you go, and be able to retire in three short years . . ."

Here, many times, during the presentation, the prospect will simply recognize how the offering would benefit him and, by the time the group presentation concludes, he will be all primed and ready to close. Other prospects in the audience won't have had these awarenesses and will not be ready to close.

So, how do you know who is who?

As closely following the conclusion of the presentation as is practically possible, sit the prospects down individually and proceed as follows:

- OPEN

- TRIAL CLOSE

If prospect shows that he is ready to close:

- CLOSE

EXAMPLE:

SALESMAN: "Hi, Chris. I'm Rick Wilson. How did you like the presentation?" (Opening)

PROSPECT: "It made perfect sense to me."

SALESMAN: "Good. Tell me something, Chris. Did our 'Just-Squeak-By' package seem more attractive to you or do you think our 'Take-The-Leap-and-Save' package would suit you better?" (Trial Close)

PROSPECT: "Rick, I'm ready to take 'The Leap.'"

SALESMAN: "Good man. This is the application form for the financing. Just start up here at the top and . . ." (Close)

If you discover that the prospect in front of you is *not ready to close*, personalize the experience as follows:

- RE-OPEN as needed by getting any objections or disagreements, particularly with the seminar itself. (Be sure to thoroughly acknowledge and handle whatever comes up here, to get your prospect into good, open communication.)

- QUALIFY—Get the Key Motivation (his main reason for possibly needing your product).

- PRESENT—Convincingly show how your product will fulfill his want(s) or need(s) until the prospect has developed a strong interest to acquire it.

- CLOSE

EXAMPLE:

SALESMAN: "Hi, Debbie. I'm Rick Wilson. How did you like the presentation?" (Opening)

PROSPECT: "The only part I didn't care for was the speaker saying that the program needed to be prepaid." (Objection)

SALESMAN: "Wow! I wouldn't like that either, after the advertising stated 'Very low investment'. What the speaker should have made more clear is that only the 5% deposit needs to be prepaid. The balance can be financed." (Reopening by acknowledging and handling objections to the seminar)

PROSPECT: "Oh! That sounds a LOT better. Come to think of it, he did say something about that. Anyhow, if all you need is 5% to get going, I might be interested.

"My not understanding enough about how to use the Internet has been the single greatest stumbling block I've had to future expansion." (Her Key Motivation)

SALESMAN: "I sure do understand that. You're not alone there. Well, as the speaker said, the single biggest benefit you can expect to get from our package is a greatly increased understanding of and ability to profit from the Internet. Here, look at a couple of these recent testimonials . . ." (Presenting how the product will fulfill the prospect's greatest need and want)

PROSPECT: "I'm sold. Sign me up."

SALESMAN: "How do you spell your last name, Debbie?" (Close)

• • • • •

As a salesman, you will find yourself in many situations which come at you "out of order." Sometimes you'll recognize exactly what is occurring and know precisely what to do about it, while other times you won't know what the heck you've been hit with and have only the guidelines and procedures in this chapter, your ready wits, and perhaps a helpful teammate or two, to improvise as effective a handling as you can.

Your best bet at all times is to:

- Stay alert;

- Use your head; and

- Do everything it takes to stabilize the confusion and get the sale back on track.

The road to Super Salesmanship has an unexpected curve in it, here and there, along the way. But as long as you use agility and care, you'll find yourself able to master the confusion and navigate even the sharpest of turns.

Super Summary
It's Out of Order

- Remain alert for prospect attempts to jump the sale to a step earlier or later than the one you are on.

- Be constantly prepared for your prospect to offer up additional qualifying data.
  - Be willing to use the fresh incoming data to modify your presentation and close.

- When your prospect *appropriately* attempts to move the sale forward, go with the flow.
  - When your prospect gives you a closing signal, cease all other activity and proceed directly into the close.

- When your prospect *inappropriately* and prematurely attempts to move the process forward, retain control and keep the sale running through its proper sequence.
  - If uncertain of the appropriateness of the move, use more questions to get the situation clarified.

- When you discover your prospect has slipped back to an *earlier* step than the one you thought the two of you were on:

1) Locate which earlier step it is that is incomplete;

2) Return to that earlier incomplete step;

3) Complete that step; and

4) Move forward to complete the sale.

- *Any* time you are uncertain what to do next: Ask-a-Question!

- Following a group presentation, retrace earlier steps as needed and close.

- Stay alert, use your head, and stabilize confusion as needed to keep the sale on track.

11

REPEAT BUSINESS

While much of your sales efforts may need to be concentrated on attracting new, first-time customers, it is a very rewarding pursuit to dedicate part of your time and energy to the development and maintenance of "Repeat Business".

You've just successfully completed your sale, during which you have won your customer's trust. The trust of a satisfied customer is an awfully valuable thing to have won. Now, by cultivating that relationship into the future, you can continue to enjoy the fruits of your labor in the form of repeat and referral business.

THE PLAN

A workable plan of action is needed to keep the relationships with your potential repeat customers healthy and productive.

> ***It is vital to keep in periodic communication
> with your client base.***

A good mix of live communication and regular written communication should be part of every game plan.

WRITTEN COMMUNICATION

A periodic (typically monthly or quarterly) newsletter or magazine is excellent, in addition to some direct mail promotion and an occasional personal letter or greeting card. To execute this part of the plan, you'll need an accurate personal contact file (see below).

LIVE COMMUNICATION

When opening a face-to-face or telephone communication with an established client, it's a good idea to show care, interest and a helpful attitude by beginning with a rudimentary "checkup."

Is He Receptive?

It is risky business to take it for granted that your relationship and the client's mood are just as good as they were the last time you were in contact.

He may be in the middle of an upset or temporarily troubled by something which may or may not have anything to do with you. It's therefore a good opening policy to

> *Keep your feelers out and inquire as needed to be sure your client is currently in a receptive mood*

and that your relationship with him is still healthy.

If you discover that there is some upset or trouble sitting there, you had better address whatever it is and get it sufficiently out of the way before trying to proceed to the "new business" portion of the program.

EXAMPLE:

SALESMAN: "You sound a little troubled. Is everything all right?"

CLIENT: "No. As a matter of fact, everything is not all right. Your last delivery came ten days late."

SALESMAN: "Oh. I wasn't aware of that. That's not okay. You deserve our very best service and I'm going to make sure that's what you're getting. Let me look into this and find out what happened so we can make sure it doesn't repeat. Anything else on your mind?"

CLIENT: "No. Everything else is fine. My customers love your new line of products and . . ."

Requirements Changed?

Another thing that may have changed is the client's requirements.

> ### *Make sure you are up-to-date on his needs, wants and don't-wants.*

Be alert for any possible changes in this area.

Product Changes

Similarly, if there are any changes in your product line or services which might affect your client, be sure to give him a full and proper presentation of them. Bearing in mind his particular needs, emphasize how any modifications to your line might benefit him specifically:

> SALESMAN: "By the way, Tim, we've increased the speed on the upgraded XL4 model which might be the perfect solution to the production bottleneck you were mentioning last week . . ."

Old Clients/New Closes

And don't take it for granted that your old established clients will automatically buy every new product you introduce to them. You may need to rehandle some old objections or possibly handle a fresh objection or two before they will close on the new product or service.

> CLIENT: "Well, the new XL4 sounds interesting all right, but for *that* much more money, I'm not completely sold. What else can it do for me that my current model doesn't?"

PERSONAL CONTACT FILE

For salespeople who have a great many clients or who generally have a limited memory for fine details (which is probably just about all of us), an excellent tool to create and maintain is a "Personal Contact File."

A separate record can be kept for each client, listing things like:

- Full contact information, including address, phone, e-mail, cell phone, etc.;
- What they bought and when;
- Key neededs and wanteds;
- Things to avoid;

- Strong interests;
- Names of people and things of importance;
- Dates of significance; and
- Notes on what transpired during the last contact(s).

> ***Reviewing your personal contact file just prior to making your next contact can be an invaluable aid in building and maintaining rapport.***

EXAMPLE:

SALESMAN: "So, how did you and Claire enjoy the golf tournament at Eagle's Grove last month?"

CLIENT: "We loved it, Bob. Nice of you to ask. I think you would have enjoyed it a lot. Maybe you'll join us for the next one . . ."

Although several excellent computer software programs are available to smartly manage this sort of information for you, starting out with a simple file box and stack of index cards will also work.

An established client should be regarded as a highly valued asset, very well worth the extra effort it takes to keep your relationship with him healthy and productive.

The path to Super Salesmanship winds its way through skillfully cultivated gardens, within which existing relationships are caringly nurtured.

SUPER SUMMARY
Repeat Business

- Keep in regular, periodic communication with your client base.

  - Send monthly or quarterly newsletters.

  - Send occasional:

    - Direct mail promotions

    - Personal letters or greeting cards

- Open all face-to-face and telephone communications with a rudimentary "checkup."

  - Keep your feelers out and inquire as needed to confirm that your client is receptive (has his attention free in general and is not upset with you).

  - Address anything you find sitting there sufficiently enough to free his attention before proceeding on to new business.

- Stay alert for any changes in a client's needs and wants.

- Keep clients briefed on any changes in your line of products or services which might affect them.

- Be prepared to do a full handling if you intend to close your client on any new products.

- Create, maintain and use a "personal contact file."

Conclusion

I think you'll agree that the knowledge and proper application of the principles in *HOW TO SELL – Clear and Simple*, as you have just studied them, will enhance the abilities of nearly anyone to close more sales, discover and exceed their customers' expectations, and build a good base of repeat and referral business.

Super salesmanship is a system in which everybody wins. The customer gets the goods and services he needs to enhance his life, the salesman gets the satisfaction and rewards which success brings, and the sales organization gets an increase of sales and future business.

YOU CAN DO IT

It is not a matter of "luck" or "natural talent" that makes a salesman a long-term success. It is a matter of finite skills and winning attitudes that can be learned and perfected.

Some people start out on the road to sales already endowed with personality traits, skills and experiences which more easily qualify them for success in sales. Others start out with fewer or none of these advantages. They can, nonetheless, as I have personally observed and experienced, still develop all that is needed to be a successful salesperson.

One's potential is vastly beyond what is commonly imagined, and training methods are currently available that are powerful enough to move even the least qualified toward success.*

THE THEORY AND THE PRACTICE

I encourage you to review the theory of selling, as covered in this book, as often as you might need or wish to in order to increase your familiarity with and certainty of these principles.

You might additionally wish to avail yourself of further theoretical materials which deal in more depth with one or another of the steps of the sales process or the "People Skills" which underlie them. Please use the questionnaire at the end of this book to let me know of your further interests.

THE SKY'S THE LIMIT

It is the knowledge of the basic principles of selling, along with an ability to apply them, that empowers a person to creatively develop and effectively correct his own sales skills, as well as to manage the sales skills of others.

To what lofty heights *you* eventually soar will be limited only by how diligently you devote yourself to the development and perfection of the techniques of the five steps of a sale and to the underlying "People Skills," upon which the selling skills—and all human relationships—are based.

---

* For more data on available training and opportunities to develop the underlying People Skills, please check these off on the Reader Questionnaire at the end of this book and get the form back to me.

From this point forward, you will become as super a salesperson as you master the technology and dedicate yourself to applying it.

Please let me know how this book helps you increase your sales, your power of persuasion, and the amount of fun you're having. At the back of this book, you'll find a tear-out page you can use to communicate your successes. I look forward to hearing from you.

Please address all correspondence to:

Harry Frisch
℅ Sales Technology International
411 Cleveland Street, Suite 245
Clearwater, FL 33755
Harry@STIPublishing.com

BIBLIOGRAPHY

of references from the works of L. Ron Hubbard

1 Excerpted from the article, D.E.I. EXPANDED SCALE (with a Note on Salesmen), 13 October 1959, in the section, SALESMAN SUCCESS.

2 Excerpted from the article, SANITY, 19 May 1970.

3 Excerpted from the article, REGISTRATION PGM NO. 2, 5 July 1974.

4 Excerpted from the article, EXECUTIVE SUCCESS, 19 March 1982.

5 Excerpted from the article, HOW TO INTERVIEW PEOPLE, 23 February 1959.

6 Excerpted from the tape lecture, R-FACTOR, TALK TO REGISTRARS, 2 February 1959.

7 Excerpted from the article, PROMOTION, 19 September 1979.

8 Excerpted from the article, DISSEMINATION TIPS, 15 September 1959.

9 Data regarding making the product real, avoiding misunderstood words and introducing the product gradiently to your prospect, are based upon educational principles contained in the article, BARRIERS TO STUDY, 25 June 1971R, Revised 25 November 1974.

10 Excerpted from the article, CREATING SURVEY QUESTIONS, 7 January 1972R Issue II, Revised 10 September 1988.

11 Excerpted from the article, D.E.I. EXPANDED SCALE (with a Note on Salesmen), 13 October 1959, in the section, SALESMAN SUCCESS.

12 Excerpted from the article, DISSEMINATION TIPS, 15 September 1959.

13 Article, TONE SCALE IN FULL, 25 Sept 1971RA, Revised 4 April 1974.

14 CHART OF HUMAN EVALUATION, in the book, *Science of Survival*, 1951.

15 Excerpted from the article, DELIVER, 28 February 1965.

16 Excerpted from the article, EXCHANGE, ORG INCOME AND STAFF PAY, 10 September 1982.

17 Excerpted from the article, COPYWRITING, 26 September 1979.

18 Excerpted from L. Ron Hubbard's Definition Notes for ACKNOWL-EDGEMENT, in the book, *Technical Dictionary*, 1975.

19 Excerpted from the article, DUMMY AUDITING, 1 December 1958.

20 Excerpted from the book, *Modern Management Technology Defined*, 1976.

21 Based upon an excerpt from the article, COPYWRITING, 26 September 1979.

22 Based upon an excerpt from the article, D.E.I. EXPANDED SCALE (with a Note on Salesmen), 13 October 1959, in the section, SALESMAN SUCCESS.

23 Based upon an excerpt from the article, D.E.I. EXPANDED SCALE (with a Note on Salesmen), 13 October 1959.

24 Excerpted from the chapter, HANDLING THE CONFUSIONS OF THE WORK-A-DAY WORLD, in the book, *Problems of Work,* 1956.

25 Excerpted from the article, RICHES OR POVERTY, THE QUALITY OF THE DISSEM DIVISION, A DISSEM DIV CHECKLIST FOR QUALITY, 15 January 1972RC, Revised 10 September 1990.

MAILING LIST REQUEST / READER QUESTIONNAIRE

Your input is important to us. When you are done reading *HOW TO SELL – Clear and Simple,* please fill out this Reader Questionnaire and mail it back to us. We value your opinion.

1. **What person or business recommended this book to you?**

2. **What did you find most valuable about *HOW TO SELL – Clear and Simple*?**

3. **How has reading it helped you so far in your professional/personal life?**

4. **If you were to describe this book to someone else, what would you say?**

5. **On which area(s) would you like additional information?** (check as many as you like)
   ☐ Prospecting ☐ Sales promotion ☐ Opening ☐ Qualifying ☐ Presenting ☐ Closing
   ☐ Objection handling ☐ Follow-through ☐ Repeat business ☐ The Emotional Tone Scale
   ☐ Increasing communication skills ☐ Handling barriers to study ☐ Hiring the right salespeople
   ☐ Super sales training ☐ Other: _____

6. **How would you enjoy receiving this information?** (check as many as you like)
   ☐ Books ☐ Audio cassettes ☐ Videos ☐ Seminars ☐ Newsletters ☐ Consulting ☐ Courses
   ☐ Other: _____

7. **You are a:**
   ☐ Sales professional ... Product line(s) _____ Years in sales _____
   ☐ Sales manager ...... Product line _____ Number of sales staff _____
   ☐ Business owner ..... Type of business _____
   ☐ Other .... Type of vocation/profession _____

ADDITIONAL COMMENTS, SUGGESTIONS, REQUESTS, QUESTIONS:

Please fill in the section below and we'll put you on our Mailing List to keep you informed of other products and services as they become available. (We respect your privacy and promise to NEVER give or sell your info to anyone else, without your prior permission.)

Name _____ Company _____
Address _____ Title _____
City _____ State _____ ZIP/Postal Code _____
E-mail _____ Country _____

Thank you for your input. Please detach from book and fax to (888) 727-9992, or (727) 466-6515, or fold so our address is on the outside, tape closed, stamp and mail. You can also e-mail us at Response@STIPublishing.com

_____

_____

_____

TO: Harry Frisch
Sales Technology International
411 Cleveland Street, Suite 245
Clearwater, FL 33755

Successes I've had reading and applying the material in this book.

(Use additional sheets if necessary.)

Name _____ Date _____

City _____ State _____

OK to publish? ☐ Yes ☐ No

Contact data: Phone (_____) _____ E-mail _____

Detach from book and mail to:

Harry Frisch

SALES TECHNOLOGY INTERNATIONAL

411 Cleveland Street, Suite 245, Clearwater, FL 33755

Or e-mail: Harry@STIPublishing.com

_____

_____

_____

TO: Harry Frisch
Sales Technology International
411 Cleveland Street, Suite 245
Clearwater, FL 33755